ADVANCE PRAISE

"A glorious celebration."

—Dan Barker, author of *Life Driven Purpose: How an Atheist Finds Meaning*

"Over the years, and through a variety of publications, Greta Christina has helped us better understand atheism and atheists. With *The Way of the Heathen* Greta has done it again. Greta's hallmark insights, biting humor, and straight-talk will lead you through some of the most important issues and practices shaping what it means to be an atheist in the 21st century. But, whether you are an atheist, a theist, or something in between, this book provides 'aha moments' that will challenge and inspire. You really should read it. I recommend it highly."

—Anthony B. Pinn, author of *Writing God's Obituary: How a Good Methodist Became a Better Atheist*

"Another bright gem from Greta Christina—an engaging, conversational, thoughtful, frank, funny, and ever timely exploration of life lived well without religion. The array of topics addressed is as impressive as the pervasive insights throughout."

—Phil Zuckerman, author of *Living the Secular Life*

"Quick-paced irresistible logic laced through with Greta Christina's humor, practical compassion, and love of life. In *The Way of the Heathen*, Greta Christina tackles topics that should feel like life's homework—justice, meaning, morality, death, love, struggle and sexuality—and somehow, by working her quirky magic, turns them into chunks of bedtime reading without losing nuance or depth."

—Valerie Tarico, Ph.D., author of *Trusting Doubt: A Former Evangelical Looks at Old Beliefs in a New Light*

"Whether it's politics, sex or Morris dancing, Greta Christina has the answers you've been searching for and the ones you didn't know you needed. She offers a succinct guide to life as a nonbeliever, describing all the joys and all the trials you're likely to face, from the mundane to the cosmic, and gives her patented and pithy wisdom on what to do when you're in the midst of them. Whether you're a baby atheist or a secular elder, you'll find something here to amuse, enlighten, or change the way you think."

—Adam Lee, author of *Daylight Atheism*

"Engaged from the first page. While *The Way of the Heathen* abounds with anecdotes and analogies, what I take away most is Greta Christina's nuanced, down-to-earth, around the breakfast table with a cup of coffee manner of speech. As with her previous books, *The Way of the Heathen* speaks TO YOU, not at you—a gift not often bestowed upon readers by atheist authors. The book is dense with facts, but Greta Christina's handling of scientific data and philosophical questioning doesn't go over your head but instead moves you to question your current perspectives and beliefs in an abrupt but non-confrontational manner. It is an easy to read book that will challenge you in the most unexpected ways, whether you are a secularist, believer or somewhere in between."

—Bridgett Crutchfield, President and Founder, Black Nonbelievers of Detroit

"If you are a newcomer to atheism in America in the twenty-first century you will be glad to spend time with Greta Christina in her new book *The Way of the Heathen*. Written with clarity and humor, the book tours some of the key issues facing someone who has recently emerged from a life defined by Christian belief. Christina roots her exploration in her own experience of awakening from religious dogma, and her candor is one of the particularly strong aspects of this much-needed work."

—Jennifer Michael Hecht, author of *Doubt: A History*

"If Richard Dawkins is best known for helping people figure out that they are atheists, Greta Christina is the community's leader who holds their hand from that point forward. Following up on her thorough guide on *Coming Out Atheist*, she now offers an exploration of how to take that secular identity and apply it throughout a person's life. *The Way of the Heathen* covers everything from a person's day-to-day experiences and interpersonal interactions to the universe's big questions and the most vexing moral, political, and social justice issues facing 21st Century society. What's great is that Christina doesn't tell the reader exactly what to think, but offers a convincing perspective from which to orient their own positions. This is the perfect book for anyone who has gotten a taste of skepticism and now hungers to make even more meaning out of their brief existence—despite living in a world that privileges religious beliefs and practices."

—Zack Ford, LGBT Editor, ThinkProgress.org

"This is the best atheist book I've read. And no, I'm not just saying that because Greta and I are friends. How do atheists find meaning? How do we cope with death? Why does atheism demand social justice? Many books eloquently criticize religion, but far fewer attempt to tackle these types of tough questions. *The Way of the Heathen* doesn't claim to be an atheist bible, but it does share invaluable insights and forces you to think deeply about a variety of difficult topics. Complete with Greta Christina's sharp wit and humor, this thought-provoking book is a must-read for people all over the religious spectrum."

—Matthew Facciani, sociologist and activist

"An indispensible, fresh, fearlessly honest guide for new atheists, not-so-new atheists, and questioning believers for wrestling with the big questions, fighting the good fight and living the good life in our wonderful, terrible universe. From the subatomic world of the quarks in the atoms of your index finger to the enormous gigantitude of the known universe, take Greta's hand and come learn why Augustine was full of crap, how to fall in love the atheist way, what 'Spock's Brain' can tell us about religion, and the joy of creating meaning in your life."

—David Fitzgerald, author of *Nailed* and *The Complete Heretic's Guide to Western Religion* series

THE WAY OF THE HEATHEN

THE WAY OF THE HEATHEN

Practicing Atheism in Everyday Life

GRETA CHRISTINA

PITCHSTONE PUBLISHING
Durham, North Carolina

Pitchstone Publishing
Durham, North Carolina 27705
www.pitchstonepublishing.com

Portions and sections of this book have previously been published in various outlets, including AlterNet, Free Inquiry, The Blowfish Blog, Greta Christina's Blog, The Humanist, or given as a talk. For a full accounting of where material has appeared before, please see the credits in the back matter of this book.

To contact the publisher, please e-mail info@pitchstonepublishing.com
To contact the author, please e-mail gretachristina@gmail.com

Printed in the United States of America

10 9 8 7 6 5 4 3 2 1

Library of Congress Cataloging-in-Publication Data

Names: Christina, Greta, author.
Title: The way of the heathen : practicing atheism in everyday life / Greta Christina.
Description: Durham, North Carolina : Pitchstone Publishing, 2016. | Includes bibliographical references.
Identifiers: LCCN 2016002862 | ISBN 9781634310680 (pbk. : alk. paper)
Subjects: LCSH: Atheism. | Conduct of life.
Classification: LCC BL2747.3 C4747 2016 | DDC 211/.8—dc23
LC record available at http://lccn.loc.gov/2016002862

Cover design by Casimir Fornalski, casimirfornalski.com

For Ingrid.

TABLE OF CONTENTS

INTRODUCTION

So You've Decided to Be an Atheist

So you've decided to be an atheist.

Okay, that's silly. No, you didn't "decide" to be an atheist: you decided to ask questions, look at evidence, prioritize reality over wishful thinking, and quit pushing your doubts to the back burner. And you've concluded that there are no gods. We don't "decide" what to believe: atheists can't decide whether we believe in God, any more than we can put our hand over a flame and decide whether we believe in heat. But we can ignore doubts and difficult questions—or follow our ideas to their logical conclusion. You've done that. And you've come to the conclusion that there are no gods—not Jehovah, not Shiva, not Zeus. Zip squat in the "gods" department.

What now?

Living without religion is not always so different from living with it. Atheists and believers are all human: we laugh at jokes, listen to music, care about our loved ones, get angry at injustice, grieve when people die, try to be good.

But there are real differences. When you think the meaning of your life is handed to you by Zeus or whoever, you're going to live differently than if you think we create our own meaning. When you think God is your co-pilot and your life is planned by this perfect, all-knowing creator (who still gave you sinuses for no apparent reason), you're going to live differently than if you think nobody's driving the bus and you'd better grab the wheel. When you think you and your loved ones are going to live forever in a blissful afterlife where everyone somehow magically gets along, you're going to live differently than if you think this short life is our only one. There are differences between a religious life and a godless one, and they're not trivial.

These differences can be unsettling, whether you've just started questioning religion, or have already rejected it and are grappling with non-belief. Even if you've been an atheist for a while, these questions may trouble you. Many atheists were brought up with religion, and were brought up framing life and death in religious terms. Many customs, rituals, and daily habits are rooted in religion, so when atheists reject these, we often don't know how to replace them. When we're confronted with a situation that our culture typically handles with religion—birth, death, marriage, coming of age, suffering, gratitude, sneezing—we sometimes feel stymied.

This book may help.

I'll get this out of the way right now: Yes, the title is a joke. There are approximately 57,852 books titled *The Way of the Something*: *The Way of the Pilgrim*, *The Way of the Master*, *The Way of the Warrior*, about 57,849 more. This title is a slightly snarky joke at the whole idea of one person telling another, "Here's the one right way to live your life." A more accurate title (although a crappier and less funny one) would be *Some Ways of Some Heathens.* If you disagree with some of this book—awesome. Ten years from now, I probably won't agree with all of it. I want people to think for themselves, using the best evidence, rationality, and compassion they can muster. There isn't a right way to be an atheist, and this is not an atheist bible: take what you need, and leave the rest.

This book is aimed at—well, pretty much anyone, atheist or otherwise, who's interested in atheism. But in particular, it's aimed at four groups:

1) Recent atheists, who have just let go of religion and are figuring out how to live without it;

2) Not-so-recent atheists, who let go of religion a while ago but want some new ideas on living as an atheist;

3) Doubting believers, who are questioning religion but are reluctant to let go, and want some ideas about how they might live without it;

4) Curious believers, who aren't having doubts but want to understand atheism better.

But what does "living as an atheist" even mean? Being an atheist just means you don't believe in any gods—why should it say anything else about you? Well, conclusions have implications. The conclusion that disease is caused by germs and not demons; that life evolved naturally instead of being poofed into existence by a god; that there are no gods paying attention to every detail of our sex lives; that consciousness comes from our brains and we die forever when our brains die—all these ideas have implications. Conclusions don't exist in a vacuum, and that includes the conclusion that gods don't exist.

So for some of us, atheism doesn't just mean, "I don't believe in God." It also means the values and ways of life implied by that conclusion, or inspired by it. (Some people use "humanism" to mean this: by all means, use that word if you prefer.)

For some of us, atheism means the ways of thinking that made us nonbelievers in the first place: a set of tools for critical thinking, an understanding of cognitive biases and how the mind works, a respect for truth over wishful thinking. (Some people use "skepticism" to mean this: by all means, use that word if you prefer.)

And for some of us, atheism means the communities, organizations, and movements springing up among people who don't believe in gods, to give each other support and advocate for our rights. (Some people use "organized atheism" to mean this: by all means, use that term if you prefer.)

For some of us, atheism is more than a conclusion. All these values, thinking skills, and community-building efforts—they're a practice. A discipline, even.

You might want some ideas about how to do it.

You might want some ideas about rooting your everyday life in the acceptance of reality. You might want new approaches to being a good person, with no rulebook supposedly written by God, and no gods to hand out justice. You might want suggestions on how to manage illness, suffering, mortality, and grief, without belief in a supernatural being who'll make everything okay. You might want strategies for participating in the atheist community, or handling relationships with believers. You might want insights into sex, love, work, joy, wonder, and transcendence, in a brief, finite, wildly improbable life.

If so—you've come to the right place. Enjoy the book!

WHAT DOES IT ALL MEAN?

CHAPTER ONE

Caring about Reality: Why It Matters What We Don't Believe

What's the point of a worldview that's about *not* believing in something?

When I talk about religion and why I think it's wrong, I sometimes get exhorted by believers to be a little more open to the universe. I've been told that "a belief system based on what *isn't* seems reductive," and that, "When I turn my mind toward the things I don't believe in, my world gets smaller."[1]

I do have a belief system. Every atheist I know has a belief system. We have values and priorities that shape how we live. So why is *not* believing in things—gods, souls, the supernatural—so crucial to that worldview?

Because I believe in reality.

I believe reality is far more important, and far more interesting, than anything we could make up about it. And trying to understand reality is one of the most valuable things we can do.

The real universe is magnificent, fascinating, and far weirder than anything we could make up about it. Space that bends? Continents that drift? Brain goop that makes consciousness? Solid matter that's mostly empty space? That rocks my world. And we've found all this out by letting go of preconceptions, and rejecting ideas that aren't supported by evidence.

But that's the thing. The negative part of this process is crucial. We can't say, "Yes, the earth orbits the sun, who'da thunk it?" without also saying, "No, the sun does not orbit the earth." We can't say, "Yes, the continents are moving, isn't that wild?" without also saying, "No, the continents are not fixed in place." We can't say, "This stuff is almost certainly true," without saying, "That other stuff is almost certainly not true."

There is an impossibly huge infinitude of things we could imagine about the universe. Only the tiniest fraction are actually true. If we're going to be open to the mind-altering magnificence and freakiness of reality, we have to be willing to say no to the overwhelming majority of things we can imagine about it. We have to be rigorous in sorting reality from unreality—and relentless in rejecting unreality.

Yes, I'm open to the universe. That's what convinced me there were no gods and no supernatural world. That was tough. I was deeply attached to my spiritual beliefs—especially my belief in a soul that survives death. I don't like death any more than anyone else, and accepting mortality was among the hardest things I've had to do. But reality wins. The carefully gathered, rigorously tested, relentlessly cross-checked evidence about the universe wins out over my biased, demonstrably flawed wishful thinking about it.

I have no problem with stories about imaginary realities. Literature, movies, television, scary stories told at a slumber party, are all important and wonderful. Made-up stories can help us frame our experience and give it meaning; they can give us fresh perspectives and help us see new things. Stories and imagination are essential parts of our human lives—and besides, they're just fun. But if we care about reality, we need to not fool ourselves into thinking our stories are true. We need to distinguish between our stories about the universe and what the universe is saying about itself.

Our world does not get bigger when we value our experience of reality more than reality itself. It doesn't get bigger when we treat every possibility as equally likely, and choose between them based on which ones we like best. It doesn't get bigger when we hang onto beliefs that are almost certainly untrue, clinging to the gossamer-thin thread that they might be true and can't be disproven with absolute certainty. It doesn't get bigger when we ignore or deny evidence. It doesn't get bigger when we armor ourselves against reality.

Our world gets bigger when we let reality in. It gets bigger when we pay careful attention to reality, and let it take priority over our opinions about it. Our world gets bigger when we let reality be what it is.

And reality is what I believe in.

CHAPTER TWO

Skepticism as a Discipline

Why does skepticism matter? When we're living our everyday lives, why should we care if the things we believe are true?

When I write about atheism, there's a response I often get: "What difference does it make if religion is true? Religion makes people happy. It gives comfort in troubling times, it offers a sense of purpose, it lets people tolerate the idea of death. If it's useful, who cares if it's true?"

My first response is always bafflement. What do people even mean when they say they "believe" something without thinking it's true? And do I really have to defend the idea that truth matters? But this is clearly a sincere question for a lot of people—so sure, I'll take it on. Why does skepticism matter? Why should we prioritize good evidence and rationality over wishful thinking and preconception? Why should we care if the things we believe are true?

Letting Go of Glucosamine

I have a chronically bad knee, and used to take glucosamine for it. I'd heard good things about it, and early research was promising—but that research didn't pan out. I was so disappointed: it had felt good to think I was doing something useful for my knee, it was comforting and gave me a feeling of control. So at first I ignored the new research. I stuck my fingers in my ears, and kept doing what I'd been doing.

But because I was beginning to identify as a skeptic, I couldn't keep it up. I couldn't ask other people to reject the wishful thinking of religion, and still embrace my own wishful thinking about glucosamine. I had to accept that it had been a waste of money, and pitch it in the trash.

Why was it so important to give something up that gave me comfort and a feeling of control? The most obvious answer is money. Of all the arguments for skepticism, not getting swindled by con artists is high on the list. But that was a minor concern here: glucosamine is pretty cheap. More importantly, when I quit doing something that I thought made a difference, I started looking for things that actually might make a difference. When I stopped taking glucosamine, I started haranguing my doctor about getting a proper diagnosis for my knee, and getting some physical therapy. When I stopped soothing myself with the illusion that glucosamine was making me better, I took action that actually helped.

When people say it's okay to believe in the supernatural without caring if it's true, they act like they only do this with religion. When it comes to health and money, what car to buy or which job to take, of course they base decisions on the evidence! But it's not so easy to question some beliefs carefully and hang onto others because they comfort us. The habits of skepticism do not come naturally to the human mind.

But good information helps us make better decisions. It helps us understand which causes are likely to have which effects. And this doesn't just apply to health care: my views on exercise, nutrition, medicine, meditation, politics, gender, sexual orientation, and much more, have all been changed for the better by practicing skepticism as a discipline of everyday life.

Perspective as a Moral Obligation

But the discipline of skepticism goes beyond improving our own lives. It affects how we see our place in the world. And that shapes how we treat others. Perspective is a moral obligation.

When we ask why we should care if the things we believe are true, we're really asking why we should treat reality as more important than our stories about it. We're asking, "Why is the universe more important than me?"

Well, for starters: The universe is 13.73 billion years old, and it's 93 billion light years across. I am 54 years old, and I'm five foot three. Not to be ageist or a size queen—but really. When I look at those numbers, do I honestly have to ask why the universe is more important, and more interesting, than the inside of my head?

Of course the insides of people's heads are important and interesting. Look at art and literature and psychology: people's heads are fascinating, and they matter. But that's a tiny fragment of the vast, ancient, freaky complexity of existence. Giving that fragment greater priority than everything else seems like the height of arrogance. In fact, it borders on unethical. It's ethically essential to understand that our experience is not the only one; that none of us has a pipeline to the truth; that we're not the most important being in the universe. Perspective—stepping back and examining our beliefs—is more than an intellectual discipline. It's a moral obligation.

And if we want to be good people, we have to understand cause and effect. Being ethical means—well, this is a gross oversimplification, but it basically means doing things that will probably have good results, and not doing things that will probably do harm. To do that, we have to accept reality.

Look at what happens when people don't accept reality. When people operate dangerous machines without finding out how they work, they're not trying to understand reality. When people drive too fast and get into accidents, they're not accepting reality. When religious parents shame, terrorize, or abuse their gay children because they're afraid the kids will go to Hell if they don't, they're not trying to understand reality, and they're not accepting it. When people ignore reality, don't try to understand it, or willfully reject it, they can do terrible damage.

So we have a moral obligation to understand how cause and effect works; in machines, nature, sex, medicine, laws and public policy, how people behave. We have to understand the world, so we know how to act in it.

All this dovetails into one more skeptical discipline—the discipline of being present in the world.

What a Wonderful World

It's easy to walk around with our heads in a bubble. It's easy to get wrapped up in our dreams and fears, our plans and memories, our fantasies and anxieties. It's easy to tune out when we talk with people, to nod attentively while we think of what to say next. When we're having uncomfortable emotions, it's easy to distract ourselves. It's easy to shut out the world, the sometimes frightening, tedious, hurtful world, and live inside our heads. It's easy, it's understandable—and I'm trying to do it less.

I'm trying to practice being more present. I'm trying to pay attention to the street art in my neighborhood, and notice a new detail every time I walk by. I'm trying to really listen when other people talk, and let their words sink in before I decide what to say. I'm trying to let myself feel what I feel; to let go of expectations, and let experiences and people be what they are. I'm trying to stop what I'm doing, at least once or twice a day, and remember that I'm alive and conscious, here in this time and place. I'm trying to literally stop and smell the roses.

I'm trying to smile at people I pass on the street. I'm trying to notice the world around me, connect with it, and let it in.

And prioritizing what's true over what I want to be true is an essential part of that practice.

Reality is a harsh mistress. She demands our honesty. She demands our work. She demands that we give up comforts, let ourselves feel pain, accept how small we are and how little control we have. And she demands that we make her our top priority. But she is more beautiful, more powerful, more surprising, more fascinating, and more endlessly rewarding than anything we could make up about her. And we can't let her in unless we're willing to let her be who she is.

CHAPTER THREE

The Uses of Irrationality, and Its Limitations

If we care about reality, do we have to be rational all the time? What about passion, love, impulse, intuition, personal taste? What about sitting on the sofa playing with cats and watching *Simpsons* marathons until two in the morning even though we have to be up early the next day? Does caring about reality and reason mean we have to give all that up?

When I'm in debates about atheism and skepticism, I often hear, "Logic and reason aren't everything. Sometimes we have to use intuition and listen to our hearts, not just to reason and evidence. There are other ways of knowing." It drives me up a tree. It's not that this idea is flatly ridiculous—there's truth to it, important and valuable truth. It drives me up a tree because that truth is being borked.

There are absolutely areas of life where logic and reason don't apply—or don't predominate, anyway. Love is the classic example: nobody decides who to fall in love with by coolly evaluating the pros and cons. Nobody decides who to fall in love with at all. It's an emotional, impulsive, largely unconscious act. Sure, some people would benefit from a *little* more rationality in their love lives: it might stop them from making the same damn mistakes again and again. But ultimately, decisions about love are made with the heart, not the head. I wouldn't want it any other way.

Or take art. The part of us that loves music, images, stories—it's not a logical part. Not entirely, anyway. A huge amount of it is emotional. And it should be. Yes, there are some widely-accepted aesthetic criteria, and we can appreciate art more when we understand its history or structure. But ultimately, art moves you or it doesn't. And when it does, it's not logical. It's subjective. That's true for artists as well, most of whom say that an essential part of the creative process is getting the rational brain to shut up for a while. Art is not primarily rational—for artists or audiences.

There are oodles of examples—humor, sexual desire, friendship, sentiment and nostalgia, tastes in food. You get the drift. Many of the most central, profound human experiences are things we experience emotionally rather than rationally.

But have you noticed a pattern to these examples?

They're all matters of opinion. They're about what's personally true for us, in our own heads and hearts. They aren't about what's true in the world—the non-subjective world we all share, the one that doesn't go away when we stop looking at it. And that's where logic and evidence leap to the fore.

We know the human mind can be fooled. We're wired, for good evolutionary reasons, with cognitive biases. Among other things, we're wired to see what we expect to see; to see patterns and intentions, even when none exist; and to think we're right about everything and whatever we've done is awesome. Intuition is deeply imperfect. Yes, it can be a powerful tool for making leaps and seeing possibilities we couldn't otherwise have imagined. It can also be a powerful tool for making damn fools of ourselves. It can be a powerful tool for showing us exactly what we expect to see, or most want to see—regardless of whether it's there.

For subjective questions, these imperfections aren't that important. If you think you're in love, you are in love. If you think Radiohead is awesome and broccoli is fermented essence of death, then for you, that's true. With subjective questions, there's no real difference between what you think is true and what really is true. But in the non-subjective world, there often *is* a difference—one that can be large, measurable, and important.

So if we want to understand what's true in the real world, we need to acknowledge, recognize, and correct for that difference. When we don't, it can be disastrous. Think of all the people in history who intuitively "knew" that black people were a subhuman species, that mental illness was caused by demonic possession, or thousands of other wrong ideas that did terrible harm. Humanity's track record of answering non-subjective questions by listening to our hearts is abysmal.

If we're trying to understand reality, the best method is the scientific one. Science has been developed over the centuries to screen out bias, preconception, and human error, as much as humanly possible, to get as close to the truth as we can. Yes, intuition has inspired important scientific breakthroughs. It's also inspired a lot of useless crap. Inspiration gives scientists ideas, points them in new directions—but they need to test those ideas. And they do that as rationally as they can.

Science is far from perfect. History is full of scientists making ridiculous assumptions and driving into dead ends, and it's full of scientists doing terrible things—to black people, to queer people, to women—because of their unexamined biases. This history of factual error and moral horror is exactly why many scientists today care so much about rigor, and screen out as much bias and preconception as they can. The failures of science have overwhelmingly come, not from applying the scientific method, but from failing to apply it.

And when it comes to understanding reality, the scientific method has been a thumping success. It's vastly increased our knowledge of the world, and our ability to affect and predict it. We can send telescopes to other planets, take pictures of those planets, and send them back to our own. We can see the structures of cells. We understand how life on Earth developed. We can predict weather patterns both large and small: not perfectly, but with greater accuracy than at any time in history. We can identify, prevent, and treat diseases that were once mysterious and deadly. Our understanding of how our minds work grows stronger every day. Of course science has frontiers, debates, and unanswered questions. Science doesn't tell us the absolute truth—but it gives us a better approximation all the time.

Compare all this to religion. Religion is one of the most important intuitive "ways of knowing"—and squabbles over whose intuition is right have resulted in murder, mass murder, war, and genocide. You'd think after thousands of years of gathering intuitive knowledge about the supernatural world, religion would have given us some actual knowledge—better techniques for praying, more accurate prophecies, something. It hasn't. There's no consensus on basic issues. There's not even a method for coming to a consensus. After thousands of years of intuitively gathering "knowledge," religions haven't been able to show that the supernatural world they're squabbling over even exists. When it comes to understanding the non-subjective world, rationality wins by a landslide.

I have great respect for intuition. I've made many an important decision on a sudden, strong impulse, the rushing together of all instincts into a clear, quiet voice. Most of those decisions have been right. And the world would be a sad, dull place without irrationality. Love and art, absurdity and sentiment, passion and humor—all these make life worth living. I would hate to live in a world where nobody hung on to the stuffed animal they had as a kid; where nobody spent weeks making scrupulously accurate *Star Trek* costumes; where nobody drove for two hours to take a midnight hike in the woods. I have tremendous value for the parts of life that are irrational. I don't want to live on Vulcan.

But I don't want to live in the Middle Ages, either.

I don't want to live in a world where we think we can cure disease by touching relics of dead saints; where we think our lives are shaped by celestial battles between angels and demons; where we think women are naturally wicked because of Eve's original sin. I don't want to live in a world where we believe all these terrible ideas, and defend them ferociously, just because they're popular and seem to make sense. And I don't want to live in a world where this intuitive "knowing" is accepted as a perfectly good way to understand reality.

I care about reality. I want to understand it as best I can. I want to live in a world where we have a good, road-tested, ever-improving method for seeing reality and making sense of it.

We do live in that world. We have that method. I want us to use it.

CHAPTER FOUR

The Sweet Mystery of Life

"It takes all the mystery out of life." People often say this about atheism and naturalism. When we try to explain the world as physical cause and effect, we're trying to explain everything—and that would somehow make life bleak and empty. Without unanswered and unanswerable questions, we'd have a yearning that could never be satisfied. And when we believe in a supernatural world we can't observe or understand, it's supposed to fulfill this fundamental need for mystery.

I despise the argument from wishful thinking with the fire of a thousand suns. But for the sake of argument, let's pretend it has some validity. Let's pretend that, even though religion is mistaken, it would still be right to perpetuate it if it served a psychological purpose—like providing a sense of mystery.

We do not need religion for life to have mystery.

If you're worried that we're in danger of understanding everything about the universe, relax. That's not going to happen anytime soon. There's a huge number of unanswered questions about the physical world, some of which are profound. The two great ones of our era, in my opinion, are "what is consciousness? and "how did the universe begin?" And there are thousands more in every field of science. What's more, it's in the nature of science that when we find answers, it almost always leads to more questions. When we figured out the theory of evolution, it led to questions about how exactly it unfolds; discovering that our galaxy was one of billions led to questions about those galaxies; ditto for atoms and the subatomic world. Solving a mystery can open a world of unsolved ones.

And sometimes when we learn new things, we have to completely revise our understanding of reality and our place in it. The history of astronomy is one long story of realizing that the universe is enormous and we are not at the center of it. And atomic physics is dizzying to think about, with its discovery that most of our world is empty space, with huge gaps between the nuclei of atoms and the electrons whizzing around them. Science doesn't just give us new facts: it gives us new ways of seeing the world.

But let's pretend that someday, we come up with perfect explanations for everything, from quarks to galaxies to the universe itself. Would this mean there'd be no more mystery to life?

Consider this. We know, reasonably well, how babies are made, and we're learning more every day. Yet the fact that it happens fills me with a gobsmacked sense of mystery and awe. The more I learn about genetics and embryonic development, the more awestruck I am. Entire human beings exist, with lives and selves as vivid as mine—and they came out of nowhere! DNA and all that embryonic stuff—it made a person! Every time I look at my nieces and nephews, the fact of their existence sends chills of amazement down my spine. And that's been true for every field of science I've learned about. The more I find out, the more I'm left speechless. Understanding the world doesn't remove the mystery, except in the narrowest sense. It enhances it.

And finally: Let's say, for the sake of argument, that none of this is true. Let's pretend that the naturalist worldview will someday explain everything. And let's pretend this would be a terrible calamity that sucked all the mystery out of life. Would deliberately blocking off areas of inquiry, setting aside some questions that could never be answered, be an appropriate reaction?

Yes, unanswered questions are part of what make us human. But that's because *we like to answer those questions.* Mysteries aren't cool because ignorance is satisfying—they're cool because solving them is satisfying. So how would it help to keep some questions off-limits? Doesn't insisting that a question can never be answered have the same effect as saying it's been answered? Doesn't it shut off our restless desire to gaze into the dark and wonder what's out there—every bit as much as turning on the light? A closed door is a closed door, whether it's closed because we looked inside and now don't need to look again, or because we refuse to open it.

I think about this desire for mystery, and I keep thinking about the belief that we have a God-shaped hole in our hearts. Augustine said our hearts were restless without God; Pascal believed in a God-shaped vacuum in every heart. We have a strong emotional yearning for something more, something outside ordinary experience—and according to many believers, this proves the "something" must exist, and must be God. But yearning for something doesn't prove it's real. And there's a better explanation for why we're restless: we're wired that way by evolution. We evolved to wonder if there's better land over that mountain, a better way to dig up roots. We're wired by natural selection to explore, invent, and discover.

Augustine was full of crap. Our hearts are not restless until we find our rest in God. Our hearts are restless, period. We don't have a God-shaped hole in our hearts. We have a hole-shaped hole in our hearts.

There is plenty of mystery in the natural world. There is mystery enough for a lifetime, for a hundred lifetimes. I want to keep exploring the world as it is—a fascinating, awe-inspiring, profoundly bizarre physical realm. And I'm not going to stop shining a light on it just because some people like to be spellbound by the mystery of the darkness.

CHAPTER FIVE

Atheist Meaning in a Small, Brief Life

If there are no gods and no universal consciousness, and human existence is an infinitesimal eyeblink in the vastness of time and space—what the heck is the point?

When atheists point out that the universe is huge, inconceivably old, largely inhospitable to human life, and utterly uncaring, it can seem like a downer. Of course, the hardass response is, "Tough cheese. Suck it up. Reality doesn't care if it hurts your feelings." But is there a more compassionate, joyful answer, that doesn't amount to "Life sucks, then you die"? Yes, human life is basically an unusual chemical process on a hunk of rock, orbiting one of a hundred billion stars in one of a hundred billion galaxies. It's only been around for about two hundred thousand of the universe's fourteen billion years, and it's pretty much guaranteed to end within the next billion, while the universe expands into mostly nothingness. Your soul isn't going to live forever, and there's no god or world-soul animating the universe who cares about your little contribution. In this universe, is it possible to find meaning and joy?

Yes. But it means letting go of a big chunk of ego.

When we let go of religion, our lives can still have meaning. We just have to let go of it having meaning on an immense, universal scale.

We have to let go of the arrogant belief that the architect of the universe cares what we do. We have to scale down the sense of where our life is lived, down from the cosmic eternal scale, and onto a finite human one. Yes, the human scale is small. That doesn't make it less real.

Let's pretend that quarks and other subatomic particles have consciousness. Now, think about the quarks in the atoms of your index finger. To them, you would be as big as the galaxy is to you; as big as the universe, if I'm doing my math right. And the atheist quarks might be having identity crises because they've realized the finger doesn't care about them and doesn't know even know who they are, and their existence is on a miniscule scale compared to the fingerverse. But the subatomic scale is still real. It's still important.

It's a mistake to think size and longevity are the truest measures of importance. A five-minute dance in the park can be more important than an old parking lot that never gets demolished; a half-second with a lover can be more important than a boring job you slogged through for twenty years. Fleeting moments are as valuable as stone monuments. Fleeting moments are all we have. We should make the best of them.

In fact, when we let go of the idea of a creator or a world-soul, the whole question of which scale is important becomes moot. Without gods, the question gets reframed: Important to whom?

In a world without gods, who cares about us? We do. We care about ourselves, and we care about each other, the other flawed, confused, messy animals living on the same mortal scale. There's no immense, eternal, perfect being watching our every move, elated at our triumphs and devastated by our failures. We matter because we matter to each other, in our own short time span, on our own small scale. We make each other important.

Being an atheist doesn't mean life isn't important. It means we make our own importance. The human scale is where we live. It's what we have. And if we decide that's the most important scale, there's nobody out there to tell us otherwise.

CHAPTER SIX

Why Are We Here?

It seems like such a deep question: *Why are we here?* It's the classic Big Philosophical Question: in the movies, if you want to show that someone's a serious thinker (or maybe a pompous blowhard), you show them wrestling with it. But it isn't really a question at all. "Why are we here?" is two questions: what caused us to be here, and what is our purpose? The first is pretty straightforward—the second we spend the rest of our lives answering.

What caused us to be here? When you don't believe in God, that has a clear answer: We're here because of physical cause and effect. This planet supports life, and our ancestors survived and reproduced. It's spectacular, it's fascinating, there's a ton of detail we don't know about it—but it's not conceptually difficult.

But when you don't believe in God, the other question—what purpose do we serve?—becomes elusive. It isn't simply mysterious. It's unanswerable. Or rather, it has no objective answer. There's no creator or designer with any job for us.

Does that mean we have no purpose? No. It means we make up our own. It means we're free. And I much, *much* prefer that. I don't want my entire reason for existing decided by a manufacturer, like I'm a memory chip in some cosmic video game. I want to decide my own purpose. Lately, that purpose is connecting with other people and other living things, making the world better, being a link in the chain of history, and experiencing as much joy as I can. It's still developing.

There's a passage from *The Lathe of Heaven* by Ursula K. Le Guin that says part of what I want to say better than I can: "Things don't have purposes, as if the universe were a machine, where every part has a useful function. What's the function of a galaxy? I don't know if our life has a purpose and I don't see that it matters. What does matter is that we're a part. Like a thread in a cloth or a grass-blade in a field."

Of course we aren't quite like grass or a galaxy: we're conscious beings, social animals with morality and empathy, and that makes everything less simple. But consciousness and conscience don't give us a ready-made purpose. They're tools we use to create our own. We have the freedom, and the responsibility, to decide what our purpose is—and to act on it.

CHAPTER SEVEN

The Human Animal

In an atheist worldview, what is our relationship with nature?

In many religions, the answer to that question is clear: Our relationship with nature is that it was made for us. Animals, plants, even the sun and moon and the planet itself, were made for people to use. They were made for us to subdue; to have dominion over, as Genesis 1:28 so charmingly puts it. Every living thing on the planet—they're all one big all-you-can-eat buffet, laid out specially for the human race. (Except for poisonous things, things that are trying to eat us, and things that are useless to us.) But when we don't believe in a world designed for humans, how do we fit into nature? What's our connection with it?

A few years ago, I read Michael Pollan's book *The Botany of Desire*. It's a history of four cultivated crops—apples, tulips, potatoes, and marijuana—that looks at human relationships with plants. In the tulip chapter, Pollan talks about how some flowers evolve in response to bees and the bees' preferences. Bees are drawn to certain colors or patterns: if flowers have these colors or patterns, they'll get pollinated by bees, and they'll get to reproduce. If they don't, they won't, unless they get pollinated some other way.

And it struck me: How is that so different from human cultivation? People are also drawn to certain qualities in flowers. If flowers have those qualities, people will pollinate them, graft them, clone them. Is that so different? Is there really that much difference between human intervention in tulips' evolution, and bee intervention?

There's an important truth about people and nature that we often forget: We are animals. Human beings are an animal species, in the primate order, the mammalian class, the vertebrate sub-phylum. Yes, we're animals with an unusual ability to shape our environment. But other living things have had dramatic effects on the planet: coral, earthworms, plants. And yes, by some definitions, humans are the dominant life form right now. But other life forms have been dominant in the past; trilobites, dinosaurs. They were around for hundreds of millions of years. We've been the dominant species for what—ten thousand years? In geological terms, we're not even a blip.

It's easy to think of humans as separate from nature. It's woven into our language and our way of thinking: nature versus nurture, natural versus man-made, is this plant native or was it brought here by people? We talk about evolution as if we were its pinnacle; we talk about the food chain as if it all headed straight into our mouths. This way of thinking even shows up in our politics and morality. When we ask if human homosexuality is born or learned or both, we often forget that we're animals—and that same-sex sexual behavior has been observed in hundreds of species. We don't think of zoology as applying to us.

I'm not saying there's no difference at all. The difference is consciousness. When it comes to tulips' evolution, we make decisions, observe which interventions make the tulips do what we want, plan how to do that more. Bees, as far as we know, don't. And that gives us a moral responsibility we wouldn't apply to other living things. Nobody would say that algae are immoral or short-sighted for overbreeding and choking a pond to death. We would say that about humans choking the planet to death. I'd say that, anyway.

But I'm reluctant to draw a bright line between humans and other animals on that basis alone. We just don't know that much about consciousness yet; what exactly it is, how it works, how the brain produces it. Until we do, I'm reluctant to say that consciousness and choice are unique to human animals. We have a long, wrongheaded history of assuming other animals don't have certain experiences—don't feel pain, don't feel attachment, have no innate morality—simply because they don't have language and can't tell us about it. And even if human consciousness is unique, it's still a product of our brains, which were produced by the natural process of evolution.

So what is humanity's relationship with nature?

Humanity's relationship with nature is that we are part of it.

We are an animal species, in the primate order, the mammalian class, the vertebrate sub-phylum. We are a product of evolution. Even the things we do that seem most unnatural—building museums, building strip malls, belching greenhouse gases into the air, sending rockets to the moon, buying bras on the Internet—are no more unnatural than coral building a reef, earthworms turning rocks into soil, algae blooming in a pond, or plants belching oxygen into the atmosphere.

I'm not saying everything we do is okay because it's natural. Plenty of things are part of nature that we'd consider immoral—rape, cruelty, biting the head off your mate. And self-preservation alone should inspire us to not act like immoral, short-sighted fools.

If anything, I'm saying the opposite. We have the capacity for consciousness—and we therefore have the capacity for foresight and choice, and the moral responsibility that comes with it. That, too, is part of our nature, a fundamental part of how our minds and social functions evolved. It's a part of our nature that has served us well. Given the power we have to radically screw up the world, our capacity for choice is a part of our nature we should embrace.

And seeing ourselves as a part of nature—not above it, not apart from it, but deeply woven into it, as deeply woven as coral and earthworms and tulips and algae—is part of that embrace.

CHAPTER EIGHT

Living Each Day as If It Were Your Last

There's an episode of *The Simpsons* where Homer is reading a book on how to be a go-getter, and he sees this piece of advice: "Live each day like it was your last." In the next scene, he's sitting on the curb, sobbing and heartbroken, crying out, "I don't want to die!"[1]

I'm sure you've all heard this at some point. It's the sort of folk wisdom that's easy to nod along with sagely, without thinking about it. And once you start thinking about it, it doesn't make any sense at all.

In the early nineties, when the AIDS cocktail first came out and people with AIDS started having a decent life expectancy, a lot of those people were suddenly stuck with a happy but not trivial problem: they'd run up enormous credit card debt. In some cases, they'd even quit their jobs. They'd been living on the assumption that they weren't going to live more than a few months or a year—and if you're not going to live more than a year, why the hell *not* run up tens of thousands of dollars in credit card bills?

They'd been living each day as if it were their last. So when it turned out this wasn't the case, and they were probably going to live for a while, they were screwed.

I guess the idea behind this folk wisdom is that you're supposed to do the things that matter to you, now, and not wait until it's too late. But what if the things that matter to you are things that take time and patience and discipline? What if the things that matter are getting a book contract or a nursing degree? Making sure your kids can go to college? Deciphering the genome of the giant panda? Winning a gold medal in badminton? Building a scale model of the Battleship Potemkin in your garage?

Let me put it this way. If I were to live each day as if it were my last, I wouldn't have spent three hours this weekend cleaning the house. I wouldn't have gotten up at 8 a.m. on Saturday to take the cat to the vet. I wouldn't try to get book contracts, or drum up publicity for the books I've already written. When I had a day job, I sure as hell wouldn't have gone to work: I liked my last day job reasonably well, but not enough to spend the last day of my life there.

But all this grunt work makes it possible to do the things I care about. I love having a home with Ingrid, a home that's a welcoming place for us and our friends and family. I love our cats. I love writing, and getting my writing into the world. And I love having food and clothes and a roof over my head. The ability to make plans and sacrifices is crucial to human happiness. We need to be able to set aside what we want right this second, so we can get something more important later. People who can't do this tend not to be very happy.

You might think that, as an atheist, living every day as if it were the last would be appealing. After all, this is our only life, and there's no pie in the sky when we die. Why not live for the moment?

I don't see it that way at all, and I don't know any atheists who do. Yes, this is our only life—so we have to make the most of it. All of it. Not just this day, but all the days we have. That doesn't mean getting twelve credits cards and running off to Amsterdam. It means doing the things that give our lives the most meaning, the things that connect us with the world and help us make our mark on it. And some of that requires patience, sacrifice, and deferred gratification.

Besides, being an atheist means being a realist. Or it should. And unless you're very old or very sick or happen to be hanging off a cliff by your fingertips, you probably have a little while yet to live. Yes, you could get hit by a bus tomorrow. But living as if that were definitely going to happen, instead of just being a slim possibility, is out of touch with reality.

If we're talking about living *in* the moment, I'm on board. It's one of the great challenges of my life—learning to get the hell out of my head and experience my life instead of analyzing it to death. But that doesn't mean cashing in my savings and buying a hot air balloon. It's a much more interesting challenge to be in the moment and fully experience life, not when we're in a hot air balloon, but when we're making dinner, or walking to work, or rubbing the cat's belly. Being fully present in the ordinary dailiness of our lives—the things that give our lives meaning even though they're not that special or exciting—that's the cool stuff.

Yes, I want this day to be a day that matters, a day I've lived fully. But chances are I'm going to be alive in a couple of years. And I want that day, two years from now, to be a day I live fully as well.

I don't want to live this day as if it were my last.

I want to live this life as if it were my last.

DOING THE RIGHT THING

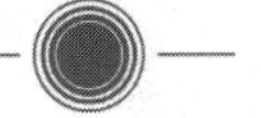

CHAPTER NINE

Two Different Ways to Be a Good Person

A friend once told me a story about someone they knew who was doing some profoundly screwed-up stuff. "The strange thing is," said my friend, "I know they think of themselves as a good person." Which of course almost everyone does. Almost nobody thinks they're a bad person. Almost nobody is a cartoon villain, rubbing their hands and cackling over their beautiful wickedness like the Wicked Witch of the West. Even terrible people think they're good people.

So I realized there are two different ways to think of yourself as a good person.

The first is by rationalizing. You think of yourself as a good person—so when you do something bad, your brain rushes in with explanations, often convoluted, for why what you did was acceptable or even virtuous. You start with the assumption that you're good, and go from there. You think of "good" as something you are, an essential part of your nature.[1]

The other way means understanding that you *aren't* always good. It means questioning and doubting; asking yourself, "Am I doing the right thing? Did I do the right thing back then? Could I have done something different?" It means understanding that being good is hard; that it sometimes involves making the least bad choice. It means trying to move closer to one end of a spectrum. It means constantly examining what being good even means. You think of being good less as something you are and more as something you do—and thus as something more fragile.

Very few people think of themselves as evil. There's a reason our brains start rationalizing what we do as soon as we do it. There's a reason that, paradoxically, we're more likely to rationalize our behavior when we've done it a lot, when we've committed more time and resources to it, when we've gone out on a limb for it, or when we've done something truly vile. We don't enjoy thinking of ourselves as bad people. We can barely stand it. Seeing ourselves as bad is so painful, we will deny reality, cut off people we care about, even continue doing the same awful things and digging ourselves deeper into that hole, rather than admit we screwed up.

And this isn't just true of ordinary people who sometimes screw up, basically decent people who swipe office supplies or don't return emails or buy consumer goods made by exploited labor. It's true of humanity's worst villains. When you think of classic evildoers like Jim Jones or Hitler, what you see is people trying to do the right thing. They just have a profoundly screwed-up notion, to say the least, of what that means. They're trying to do the right thing by, say, eliminating the vile scourge of the Jews. And they want to impose their own vision of goodness onto people—without those people's consent, by using people as means to an end, and by killing people by the hundreds or thousands or millions. Classic evildoers aren't boasting of their wickedness and luxuriating in it. They rationalize. The use euphemisms so their talk of killing people doesn't mention killing; they use dehumanizing language so their talk of killing people doesn't mention people. They want to do good, but their ideas of what that means and how to make it happen are simplistic, coercive, dehumanizing, brutal, and murderous.

It can be comforting to externalize evil, to see it as something the bad guys do. But it's a false comfort, and a dangerous one. If we learned anything from the Milgram Experiment[2] or the Stanford Prison Experiment[3], it's that evil isn't That Thing Out There. It's a way of being. It's a capacity all of us have. We all have the capacity to be bigoted; to be corrupted by power; to obey orders or go along with the crowd even when we know it's wrong; to reflexively defend ourselves and people on our side even when we've done something awful. And we all have the capacity to hate and dehumanize people who we see as not like us.

We need to be willing to see evil, not as something people are, but as something people do. We need to be willing to see evil as something *we* might do. We need to be willing to ask, not if we're the good guys, but if we're doing the right thing. And we need to ask this again and again, for as long as we live.

This self-doubt has its downsides. It makes it easy to let the perfect be the enemy of the good. It can be immobilizing: we can get so worried about doing the right thing, it keeps us from doing anything at all. And it can lead to low confidence and low self-esteem. Self-doubt can stop us from recognizing all the ways we've done good and are doing good; it can make us obsess over how we've been weak or lazy or selfish, or simply failed. As messed-up as it can be, rationalization is essential. We'd be frozen without it.

So I keep thinking about what Hillel said: "If I am not for myself, then who will be for me? But if I am only for myself, who am I?" We have to be for ourselves if we're going to survive; we have to be for others for our lives to have value. We have to constantly tinker with that balance. And the ways we think about being good are part of that balance. If we're going to function, we have to see ourselves as good people. But if we want that goodness to be meaningful, we have to be willing, at least sometimes, to question it.

CHAPTER TEN

Good Intentions

"I didn't know that was a racist word!" "I broke your sink and flooded the kitchen—but I was trying to help!" "When I told my secretary how sexy she was, I meant it as a compliment!"

If we cause someone pain, does it matter if our intentions are good?

When we hurt someone, there are a couple of ways to say we meant well. The first is, "I didn't intend you hurt you. I'm so sorry. Here's what I meant to do—I meant to do something good, but I see that I failed, and actually did something that hurt you. I was tired, harried, uninformed, careless, and I'm really sorry. Let me know if I can undo the damage or make things better. I'll be more careful in the future."

And then there's the second: "Why are you being so mean to me? I didn't intend to hurt you. I meant to do something good—so the fact that I actually hurt you is irrelevant. I was tired, harried, uninformed, careless—so it's not fair to tell me how I hurt you and why you're angry. Let me tell you, at length, how your criticism is hurting my feelings, and how you should have said it instead."

These statements are not the same. In Statement Two, note the lack of apology; the lack of concern for the damage done; how the offender's hurt feelings are the top priority; the lack of any promise to change.

If someone steps on my foot by accident, I'll certainly be a lot less pissed off, and a lot more willing to forgive, than if they did it with malice aforethought.[1] But to forgive an unintentional injury, I need to believe that the person who hurt me gives a damn and intends to do better. They don't need to pour dirt on their head and chant "Mea Culpa" a thousand times (although if they hurt me badly I need to see some proportional concern). I just need to hear, "I'm sorry. I didn't mean to hurt you, but I understand that I did anyway. I'll work to do better in the future."

The point of saying you didn't mean to hurt someone isn't to rationalize, deflect responsibility, and make yourself feel less bad. The point is to convey regret and a desire to do better. If someone injures me, and they don't show any regret, they'll probably do it again. And that makes their intention irrelevant.

Intention is not trivial. There's a reason attempted murder is still a crime, even if nobody got killed. There's a reason some motives for killing people are considered worse than others, and some (like self-defense or defense of a bystander) aren't considered crimes at all. Intention is an important part of any moral equation. But for good intentions to have power, they have to show concern for the hurt that was done, a willingness to make things right, and a commitment to do better. Without that, good intentions are useless.

When someone is suffering, believers often say, "I'll pray for you." Many atheists make fun of this, pointing out that prayer accomplishes nothing and is literally the least you can do. It's a fair point: if someone is suffering, it's absurd to act complacent because your response was to call your invisible friend. If atheists want to do better, we can't treat good intentions as if they were magic. Nice thoughts don't, by themselves, do any good. That's true whether the thoughts are aimed at a god, or at the person we hurt.

CHAPTER ELEVEN

Starting with the Assumption That I'm Wrong

(Content note: references to ableist language)

Last year, I started doing this thing. If I'm contemplating a change in my thinking or my life, especially for ethical reasons, I shift my perspective for a bit, and start with the assumption that I'm wrong.

I don't mean this in a "proof by contradiction" sort of way, like in logic or math, where you assume that the thing you're trying to prove is wrong so you can come to a paradox and thus find out it's really right. I mean it in a practical way—living and thinking, temporarily, as if my old ideas are wrong and the new ones I'm considering are right. I mean living with the new ideas for a while, to see if my thinking gets clearer. And I mean experimenting to find out: If I were wrong, if I had to change, what would my life look like?

We all tend to start with the assumption that we're right, smart, and good. It's how our human brains work: as soon as we do a thing, we start rationalizing why it was awesome. And when we're challenged on it, we get defensive. It doesn't make us bad people: it's just part of the necessary machinery of our minds.

But when it comes to important questions that I genuinely want to examine, rationalization can be a real problem. I've been looking at ways to hijack it. And it's been helping to start with the assumption that I'm wrong, to temporarily live as if I'm wrong and need to change—and see what that looks like.

Here are two examples. A little while ago, I did a charity fundraiser on my blog where I promised that if we raised a certain amount of money, I'd go vegetarian for a month. I did this partly as a charity stunt—but I also did it as a test. For years, I've been wrestling with the ethics of meat and sliding up and down the vegetarian spectrum. I'd tried to go fully veggie before and wasn't able to sustain it—but that had been twenty years before, and vegetarianism has become easier. So I wanted to test: If I lived for a month acting as if I thought eating meat was wrong, would that change my thinking? And if I decided it *was* always wrong, what would my life look like?

It looked different. When I wasn't eating meat, and wasn't unconsciously rationalizing it, my thinking changed—both about the ethics of meat and the ease of avoiding it. I won't bore you with the details, but while I'm not a hard-core vegetarian now, I've slid much further in that direction.

A more recent example is the Ableism Challenge. On the blog *Alyssa and Ania 'Splain You a Thing*, Ania Bula asks people to go one month without using ableist language—using words for physical or mental disabilities as insults, including lame, dumb, crazy, retard, and more.[1] With a lot of this language, the problems are clear: it's obvious that using "lame" and "crazy" as insults stigmatizes disability and mental illness. But with some of this language, I was baffled. Specifically, I was struggling to find alternatives to the word "stupid"—and I didn't really understand the problem with it.

I knew, though, that if I tried to examine the question from first principles, I'd probably just rationalize what I was doing—why it was okay, why I should keep doing it, and why people trying to convince me I was wrong were doo-doo-faces. And I generally listen to marginalized people when they object to something, and take their word for it, even if I don't understand their reasoning. So I decided to just try it.

And it has changed my viewpoint. It's made me realize how much I use this kind of language without even thinking about it, and how I use it in ways that are sloppy or lazy. Discarding ableist language is occasionally annoying, but for the most part it's made my language more precise. And this experiment—and the conversations I had with myself and others about it—has made me realize that my reasons for wanting to hang on to the language were woefully inadequate. They amounted to thinking that I wanted to do this, it was easy and familiar, and this was more important than the fact that it hurt people.

I don't think I would have come to these conclusions if I'd tried to reason them from first principles. I needed to try them in the real world to see how they played out. And loosening my attachment to the old idea made it easier to examine it.

Sometimes—okay, a lot of the time—when I'm considering making a change, I have the sneaking suspicion that the real reason I don't want to change is that it's hard. Now, sometimes that's valid. If you support public transportation but you work twelve-hour days and public transit would add two hours to your commute, I think it's legit to say, "I'd like to quit driving but it's too hard." But if I'm deciding to not make a change purely because it's hard, I want that to be a conscious choice, not an unconscious bias warping my thinking. (If for no other reason: If the thing gets easier down the road, I want to take that into account. I've skewed a lot more towards the vegetarian end of the spectrum since veggie options became easier to find.)

Like Mr. Darcy in *Pride and Prejudice*, we love to think our decisions are not influenced by our hopes or fears. We love to think we believe on impartial conviction, not because we wish to. And like Mr. Darcy, we are full of it. Our thinking is *always* weighted towards the conclusion that the things we want to be true really are true. And we can't counter that bias simply by being aware of it, or by pinky-swearing that we won't succumb to it. We have to find ways to lighten our bias—or to create counterweights on the other side.

And if I want a counterweight to the assumption that I'm right, one of the weightiest ones I can think of is to assume I'm wrong—and see where it leads me.

CHAPTER TWELVE

Should We Care What Other People Think?

"Care about what other people think and you will always be their prisoner." —Lao Tzu

"Don't be trapped by dogma—which is living with the results of other people's thinking. Don't let the noise of other's opinions drown out your own inner voice." —Steve Jobs

In modern U.S. culture—and in many cultures in many ages—there's great admiration for the trailblazer, the inventor, the social reformer, for people who defy public opinion to speak the truth as they see it. If you Google the phrase "care what others think," the first page of results (as of this writing, on my computer) gives nine links and five images, all but one arguing passionately that caring what others think is a terrible idea, or giving suggestions on how not to do it. After all, the trailblazers and defiers are the ones who make history and change the world with their new ways of seeing and doing.

As a card-carrying member of the Strong-Minded Independent Thinky Person Task Force, I share that admiration. But as an independent thinker who questions truisms and social norms, I want to question this one. I understand the desire to reject conformity and defy public opinion—boy, howdy, do I understand it. But as a catch-all guideline for How We Should Always Live Our Lives, "To hell with what other people think" is far too simplistic.

As a matter of pure practicality, it makes sense at least sometimes to care what other people think. If I'm preparing for a job interview, for instance, I need to put some thought into what my potential boss will think of me. Humans are social animals: we live in an intricate piece of social machinery, we depend on others for survival and happiness, and being aware of how people perceive us is part of what makes that work. If other people see us as unfeeling and arrogant, disorganized and flaky, short-sighted and reckless, and we don't realize it or don't care, we're going to be in trouble. And when other people have power over you, you bloody well have to care what they think. In some cases, your life might depend on it. Not caring what other people think is a privilege. It's a whole lot easier when you have power, wealth, other advantages—when you have a safety net, or your life isn't in someone else's hands.

But even apart from these practical concerns, it's important, at least sometimes and in some ways, to care what other people think. It's important for one very big reason, one that should matter to atheists and anyone of a skeptical mindset:

Other people are a reality check.

I don't perceive reality perfectly. I don't know everything: in fact, I know only a tiny fragment of knowable things. And I filter my perceptions through expectations and wishes—filters that often distort. Listening to other people gives me a reality check. It gives me a clue about whether I'm overthinking or underthinking, overreacting or underreacting, being self-absorbed or not taking enough care of myself, being too abstract or thinking with the little head instead of the big one. And it gives me a clue about whether I'm doing none of these things, and am doing just fine. Of course other people aren't always right—but neither am I. Not caring what other people think would mean assuming my brain is perfect and I know everything. That's just silly.

And other people aren't just a reality check. They're a morality check. Other people are a mirror that helps us see right and wrong.

I said earlier that if we come across as arrogant, flaky, reckless, and so on, we're going to be in trouble. That's true for selfish reasons—other people won't treat us well if they think we're jerks—but it's also true for ethical reasons. If we're coming across as jerks, there's a non-trivial chance that we *are* being jerks. Human brains are wired with many cognitive biases, and some of our biggest biases are the ways we rationalize our actions and think everything we do is right. Other people can see things about us that we can't—and that's especially true when it comes to the ways we screw up. If we care about being good, if we genuinely want to know when we hurt people, we have to listen when they tell us about it. We have to care what other people think.

Of course other people aren't always right. But neither are we.

Yes, history is full of trailblazing geniuses who followed their vision despite the naysayers. History is also full of stubborn, arrogant fools who refused to listen to the people around them. It's easy to see in retrospect which is which, to see that Steve Jobs was a genius and General Custer was a genocidal fool. But in the moment we're making a decision—especially a big decision that we're making with limited or imperfect information—it's hard to know if we're being Custer or Jobs. Only time will tell, and even time can be a liar: sometimes things turn out well or badly because of plain old unpredictable luck.

So when we're trying to figure out what's true and what's right, we should listen to our own observations and instincts—*and* we should listen to other people. We should let all of this into the mix. Caring too much about what other people think can make us anxious, self-conscious, powerless: not caring enough can make us insensitive, self-absorbed, willfully ignorant. We have to find the balance. It's going to be a different balance with every decision—and we'll never know for sure if we're getting it right.

There's a bit in the final *Hitchhiker's Guide to the Galaxy* book, *Mostly Harmless*, where one of the Earth characters gets a chance to go adventuring into space. She tells the space alien to wait while she gets her handbag, he gets impatient and takes off without her, and she misses her chance. The lesson she learns from this is: When offered a unique opportunity, never go back for your bag. Later, she's offered another once-in-a-lifetime opportunity; she jumps at it; but for this opportunity, she needs her contact lenses. Which—you guessed it—are in her bag, which she didn't go back to get. To quote the book: "If there was one thing life had taught her, it was that there are some times when you do not go back for your bag and other times when you do. It had yet to teach her to distinguish between the two types of occasions."

There are times when we should care what other people think, and times when we shouldn't. And life is rarely going to be clear about which is which.

Of course we shouldn't be swayed by mindless conformity. Of course we shouldn't assume something is true just because lots of people think it. But we should also understand the limits of our knowledge, and accept the strong probability that we're wrong about a lot of things. We should understand cognitive bias and the hundreds of ways our minds deceive us. And we should embrace other people's perspectives as a lens that helps us see the world—and a mirror that helps us see ourselves.

CHAPTER THIRTEEN

Doing It Right: An Atheist View of Sexual Ethics

If we don't believe God is peeking into our bedrooms and taking notes—if we don't think there even is a God, much less one who cares who and how we boff—what do we base our sexual ethics on? Without God, are we looking at a sybaritic free-for-all, uninhibited by any constraints?

The answer, obviously, is no. Of course we have sexual ethics, and we wouldn't want it any other way. The sybaritic free-for-all can be an entertaining fantasy, but we wouldn't want a sexual world with no ethics, where nobody cared who got hurt. But without belief in God, we're free to base our sexual ethics on—well, ethics. We don't have to base them on books written thousands of years ago by people who were convinced they had a pipeline to God.

Humans evolved with some core ethical values hard-wired into our brains as a social species. And we hammer out the finer points based on the standards of our particular society—and on our own experience of what hurts and helps, what's fair or unfair, what keeps society running. That's what we can base our sexual ethics on. We don't have to worry whether God thinks anal sex is gross. Instead, we can focus on actual ethical concepts—such as consent, honesty, fairness, and harm.

To see how these ethics might play out in our sex lives, let's look at some questions religion famously has opinions about. Let's start with a no-brainer: Is homosexuality moral? Instead of replying that gay sex makes Baby Jesus cry, we can ask if it harms anyone, if it's consensual, whether same-sex relationships injure society, whether it's fair to have different rules for same-sex and opposite-sex relationships. When you look at these questions, the answers are obvious: gay sex is every bit as ethical as straight sex, and there's no reason to treat it as a special case.

Let's take another example, with somewhat less obvious answers. If we're considering the ethics of pornography and erotica, instead of looking to holy books for a thumbs-up or thumbs-down, we can ask: How does pornography affect people, and is the research about it careful or shoddy? Is there good evidence that pornography contributes to sexism and misogyny—any more than TV, movies, videogames, or other areas of pop culture? How much can we ask our partners to limit their sexual behavior, and does that change when the behavior is private? Can we acknowledge the right to freedom of expression, and still critique what porn often looks like in our culture? Does all this play out differently with different kinds of porn? When we look at these questions through secular eyes, our answers will change—and they might actually have a connection to ethics.

And if we're looking at sexual limits in a relationship, we don't have to look at God's Do's and Don'ts. We have to look at the people having the sex. Is this sex act consensual? Does everyone want to do it? Is this particular act relatively safe, or is it likely to cause harm? If it is riskier, is everyone who's involved emotionally capable of taking on that greater risk? Is everyone being honest? I'll talk more about this in the chapter on consent, but the basic principle should be clear by now: If we're considering the ethics of oral sex, anal sex, spanking, bondage, cross-dressing, multiple partners, dominance and submission, piss play, dressing up as animals, or any of the long list of items in the human sexual repertoire, we don't look at someone else's checklist to see if the acts are on it. None of these acts is inherently ethical or unethical. What makes them ethical is how we approach them.

When we look at these questions through secular eyes, some of the answers become very clear. Others become much more nuanced. A lot of sexual situations fall into gray areas where different values come into conflict, and they have to be viewed on a case by case basis. Let's look at a monogamous marriage where one spouse has decided they don't want to have sex any more. This isn't temporary, because they're sick or depressed or just had a baby: it's permanent. They're not willing to discuss the issue, go to couples' counseling, or consider non-monogamy. As far as they're concerned, the fact that they're done with sex means their partner is, too. Is this morally wrong? And would it be morally wrong for the other partner to seek sex outside the marriage? (This isn't a hypothetical: it's very common. And don't assume it breaks down along conventional gender lines—it doesn't.)

We have two conflicting ethical values here. Do people have the right to say no to sex? Of course we do. We own our bodies, and our right to self-determination about our bodies is damn near absolute. We have the right to say no to sex in general, to any particular kind of sex, to kinds of sex we've said yes to before, to people we've said yes to before, at any time, for any reason, or for no reason. And we have the right to keep saying no for as long as we want—including for the rest of our lives. But do people have the right to non-consensually eradicate other people's sex lives? I don't think so, and for pretty much the same reason: We own our bodies, and we own our sexualities. We can make agreements about what limits we'll put on our sex lives—but it's not reasonable to demand that someone turn off their sexuality permanently because of an agreement they made years ago.

You might argue that people can always leave a marriage, but what if that's *s* morally problematic? What if they have children or a business together, or one spouse is financially dependent on the other?

My point in raising this question is not to settle it. My point is that when we move away from religious taboos about specific acts and arrangements, we have to accept that a lot of situations raise questions that aren't easy to answer. We have to be willing to make difficult ethical choices, and we have to take responsibility for them.

And part of accepting responsibility is not making decisions by default. Far too many people take major steps in their sexual lives based on social consensus: people decide when to start having sex, when to move in together, when to get married, when to have kids, simply because that's the next step. "We've had five dates—isn't it time for sex?" "We've been going out for two months—isn't it time to become exclusive?" Even if we don't look to God's checklist, we look to an external timetable. And people often don't consider *whether* to take these steps at all; whether to move in together, stop seeing other people, get married, have kids, have sex at all, get into a serious relationship in the first place. Making these decisions by default is a recipe for resentment, for feeling trapped in a situation that feels like you didn't choose it—because you didn't.

So if we're not basing our sexual ethics on religious taboos or social consensus, what do we base them on? For starters, we can base them on evidence. If we're considering the issue of same-sex marriage, we have to look at the evidence about how same-sex couples affect communities, how their kids turn out, and so on. If we're pondering the ethics of porn, we have to look at the evidence about how porn affects people. Our sexual ethics have to be based in reality. We need to pay attention to good research—and we need to listen to what people say about their own sex lives. Way too many people make judgments about gays and lesbians, polyamorists, porn performers, porn consumers, transgender people, asexual people, consensual sadomasochists, sex workers, sex work customers, and so on—without ever hearing from the people themselves. That is not good sexual morality. Most atheists are sick of believers making assumptions about us without bothering to spend five minutes on Google: so we need to do some Googling ourselves, read what people say about their own sexuality, and accept that they probably know more about it than we do.

I was once in an online debate with an atheist about polyamory (being open to sexual or romantic relationships with more than one person at a time, honestly and by mutual agreement). This guy insisted that poly relationships were unequal and selfish, and he kept talking about the inequity of the "standard polyamory setup"—a harem-type arrangement of one person with multiple partners who don't have sex with each other or anyone else. Several polyamorists pointed out that there's no such thing as a "standard polyamory setup": virtually every poly relationship has a different arrangement, and the harem arrangement is actually pretty rare. But even though this guy had pulled this notion out of his own ass, he kept defending it. It was Exhibit A on how not to think about sex (or anything else for that matter). If we want to have good, reality-based sexual ethics, we need to be willing to change our minds.

We can't make judgments based on what's normal, either. If we're wondering if something is ethical, we can look at consent, honesty, fairness, harm—there's no reason to ask how many other people are doing it. And we can't make ethical judgments about sexuality purely on the basis of what grosses us out. This is a surprisingly difficult principle to grasp: religious believers tend to assume their gods are grossed out by the same things they are, but even atheists often translate personal revulsion into moral revulsion. If people are personally upset by the idea of homosexuality, polyamory, sex work, or other variations, they often jump to the conclusion that these things are immoral and nobody should do them. What helps me, if

I'm grossed out by some sex act and am feeling morally revolted as a result, is to do what I call the broccoli test.

I, personally, am revolted by broccoli. The thought of eating it makes me retch; I can barely stand to be in the room when it's being cooked. But I don't think people who do like broccoli are immoral. I don't try to talk people out of eating broccoli, or try to get laws passed banning it: I'm not out at the farmer's market every Saturday picketing the broccoli stand, chanting, "Never again!" I don't avoid friendships or relationships with people who eat broccoli: my wife eats it, and that's fine with me. And I don't try to get people who eat broccoli banned from teaching in public schools because their moral turpitude clearly renders them unfit to be in the presence of children.

In the same way, there are kinds of sex I find completely unappealing, even actively unpleasant. Take adult diaper play. This is a sexual fetish in which adults consensually dress up as babies, including wearing diapers, and enjoy various sexual activities. I'm totally turned off by it; I'm not interested in even trying it. So what? Who cares what I think? Nobody's making me do it. If the people who are doing it are consenting and happy, what business is it of mine? I don't want to do it—and I completely support people who do.

It's common to do dimestore psychology about other people's sex lives: to assume sexual masochists have guilt complexes or sex workers have poor self-esteem. But we just don't understand sexuality all that well, and trying to figure out where desires come from is like reading tea leaves in a hurricane. So apart from obviously immoral acts like rape, sexual practices are a terrible barometer of character. They tell us nothing about people, other than whether we might want to have sex with them. And whenever I forget this, whenever I'm tempted to make judgments about people because I'm grossed out by what they do in bed, I always have to remember that plenty of people are grossed out by what I do, even though I know it's consensual and harmless. So if I want other people to respect my right to make my own sexual decisions—as long as they're consensual and fair and don't hurt anyone—I need to extend that respect to other people.

Atheist sexual morality can be challenging. It requires a lot more thought than following a checklist of supposedly divine Do's and Don'ts. It requires that we look at sex, sexuality, gender, bodies, desire, and a host of other intense emotional issues, more carefully than we might be used to. It requires us to be more honest about our own sexuality, our own gender, our own bodies and desires, than we might be used to. It requires accepting the reality of nuance and non-obvious choices. It requires changing our minds, which is rarely easy.

But it has the advantage of actually being moral.

CHAPTER FOURTEEN

Consent

(Content note: rape, child rape, other violations of sexual consent)

Consent is saying yes when we have the power to say no.

That's an oversimplification, a soundbite. Sexual consent is a large topic: huge amounts have been written about it, entire books have been written about it.[1] But if I had to sum up consent in one short sentence, it would be that.

In many religions, sexual morality isn't about consent. The Old Testament famously prohibits adultery and homosexuality, while endorsing forced marriage and rape: even today, religions condemn gay people and others for enthusiastically consensual sex, while pressuring married women into having sex they don't want. Religious leaders even equate homosexuality with pedophilia: in their minds, once you abandon any of God's rules, you might as well abandon them all. It's almost irrelevant to them that gay sex is consensual and pedophilia isn't.

But leaving religion doesn't automatically rid us of religious indoctrination, and not all terrible ideas about consent come from religion. To give just one example among many: Several years ago, the atheist and skeptical communities were swept by a firestorm of controversy over sexual harassment policies at conferences—controversy that still flares up today. Opponents of the policies painted supporters as sex-hating, moralizing prudes who didn't want anyone at conferences to hook up or flirt. They treated the idea of consent as almost irrelevant: making sure sexual pursuits were consensual, requiring clear communication to make sure of that, and spelling out consequences if this didn't happen, were treated like a ban on any kind of sexy fun. This attitude is hardly new: in the sexual revolution of the sixties and seventies, sexual liberation was often equated with men getting lots of the sex they liked, without much attention to how women felt about it. If we want to unravel religious sexual morality, we need to replace it with something other than a free-for-all. We need sexual ethics that are actually ethical—and consent is the cornerstone.

Which brings me back to my soundbite: Consent is saying yes when we have the power to say no.

If someone holds a gun to my head and says they'll shoot me or beat me up unless I have sex with them, and I say yes, that's not consent. If my landlord says they'll evict me or my boss says they'll fire me unless I have sex with them, and I say yes, that's not consent. If an adult asks a child to have sex, and the child says yes, that's not consent. If a person is drunk or high to the point of being incapacitated, and they say yes to sex, that's not consent. If a person is passed out, and they don't say no because they can't speak or don't know what's happening, that's not consent.

Consent means saying yes when we have the power to say no, when nothing terrible will happen if we say no. There may be consequences we don't like—someone might not want to date us, or might break up with us—but nothing terrible will happen. We won't get shot, beaten up, evicted, fired. And the power to say no means the psychological capacity to say no. Adults have a huge amount of power over children—and that power includes the fact that children's minds are wired by evolution to listen to them, to trust them, and to do as they're told. They don't have the capacity to say no to adults. And if someone is incapacitated by booze or drugs, they don't have the capacity to consent. That's literally what "incapacitated" means.

This issue of booze and sexual consent is difficult for a lot of people. In my talks on atheist sexual ethics, and in the debates about harassment policies, the subject of alcohol almost always comes up—and someone usually asks, "How drunk is too drunk?" My short answer is to quote Rebecca Watson: if you're wondering if someone is too drunk to consent, err on the side of not being a rapist.[2] But there's more to it than that. We need to seriously question the role of alcohol in our sexual culture.

U.S. culture tends to treat alcohol as the oil of the social-sexual machinery. Alcohol loosens inhibitions, and we treat that as necessary to keep the machine of flirtation and cruising and hookups going. We see bars and drunken parties as natural places to find sex partners; our jokes and conversations and popular culture are loaded with connections between booze and sex. We tend to treat sex and alcohol as two great tastes that taste great together. We need to knock it off. I'll quote my colleague Christophe Pettus: If a large amount of your sex life consists of gray-area sex, where you're not sure if your partners are sober enough to consent, you need to re-evaluate your life. And the unfortunate reality is that alcohol is a common component of sexual assault. I don't mean that in any victim-blaming way: I'm not saying people who get drunk and are sexually assaulted should have known better and deserve what they get. I'm saying people who sexually assault others use alcohol and drunkenness as a weapon—and a defense after the fact. They know our culture sees drunkenness as a green light, and they rely on that as a way to get off the hook.

I'm not saying every flirtation or hookup or sexual encounter needs to be stone cold sober. I'm saying we need to untangle this connection between booze and sex. We need to start seeing tipsiness and drunkenness, not as a sexual green light, but as a red flag, a sign that we should proceed with caution. Again: If you're wondering if someone is too drunk to consent, err on the side of not being a rapist.

So if consent is saying yes when we can say no, what counts as saying yes? In conversations about consent, a common idea is "clear, verbal consent." Especially when we're having sex with someone for the first time or the first few times, or when we're trying a new sexual act, it's important to not just rely on body language. And it's hugely important to not assume that a silent, passive partner is consenting simply because they're not saying no. No means No; Maybe means No; silence means No. The only thing that means Yes is Yes. Getting clear, verbal consent, for sex in general and for particular sex acts, is an important part of erring on the side of not being a rapist. If it seems awkward, clinical, or unromantic to talk openly about sex, and to explicitly discuss sexual plans, boundaries, likes and dislikes—ask yourself why that is, and why our culture treats explicit consent as unsexy. Now, if you've been married for eighteen years, standing agreements are common, and clear communication doesn't always have to be verbal. That's true about lots of things other than sex. But even then, clear verbal consent is a good idea—and people *always* have the right to withdraw it. The fact that you've had sex with someone once before, ten times before, a thousand times before, doesn't mean you're consenting to have sex with them again.

Then there's the idea of "enthusiastic consent." The idea is that we don't just want our sexual partners to say, "Yeah, sure, okay." We want them to say, "Yes yes yes yes yes, yes please, hell yes, that would be awesome." Enthusiasm is a really good sign that your partner is genuinely consenting. Now, this isn't an absolute hard-and-fast rule in all sexual encounters. Many sex workers have pointed out that they aren't always enthusiastic about sex with their customers, and they're still consenting. And many asexual people in relationships with sexual people say they freely consent to have sex they're not enthusiastic about, because it's important to their partner and is an important bond. But as a general guideline for most people in most sexual encounters, enthusiastic consent is what we should be looking for. If someone's not enthusiastic, that's often a good sign that they're saying yes, not because they want to, but because they don't feel like they can say no.

So consent means saying yes when we have the power to say no. Power means literal power—not having a gun to your head or your job on the line. Power means the mental and emotional capacity to make decisions. But I would argue that consent doesn't just mean the power to say no. It means the power to say yes.

In Islamist theocracies, women can be punished by imprisonment or beating or death for having sex outside marriage. There are countries where having gay sex is a crime punishable by death. For decades in Ireland, the Catholic Church literally imprisoned women they thought were too sexual.[3] That's not consent culture, either. Punishing people for saying yes to sex chips away at consent—and that includes in the slut-shaming U.S. When we discourage people from saying yes and stigmatize them when they do, it perpetuates the idea that the way to consent to sex is with ambivalence or silence. When we shame people for having casual sex, for having unconventional sex, for having sex with too many partners ("too many" being defined as "more than we personally approve of"), we're chipping away at consent. Sexual empowerment means the power to say no—and it means the power to say yes.

If we want to create a culture where sexual consent is valued and taken seriously, we need to take a hard look at all the ways our culture doesn't do that. We need to look at how our culture thinks sex should be spontaneous and natural and beyond language; how making plans for sex, and openly discussing our likes and dislikes, is seen as awkward or cold. We need to look at how saying no or showing reluctance is seen as coy and flirtatious. We need to look at the all-too-common assumption that once someone has consented to sex, they've consented to that person forever. We need to look at how a drug that causes disinhibition at best and incapacitation at worst is seen as a natural part of rollicking dirty fun. We need to look at all the ways sexual assault is trivialized. We need to look at all the ways victims of sexual assault are mistrusted, ignored, dismissed, or blamed. We need to look at all the ways perpetrators of sexual assault are defended, and how common it is for them get away with it. We need to look at how news media commonly refers to rape or sexual assault as "sex," "sex crimes," a "sex scandal," "inappropriate sexual behavior," and other minimizing language. We need to look at all the ways we treat sexual assault as a special case; how even police and prosecutors are less likely to believe rape victims than victims of other violent crimes, and more likely to blame them for having been raped. We need to look at how the very idea of rape culture is seen as absurd, and any instance of rape being taken seriously is given as proof that it doesn't exist.

And we need to look at all the ways that boundaries in general are not taken seriously. We need to look at all the ways our culture sees not asking for consent—not just for sex, but for kissing or touching or dancing—as passionate and impulsive. We need to look at all the ways we think persistence and not taking no for an answer—not just for sex, but asking someone for a date a hundred times—is cute and romantic and a sign of true love. We need to look at how children are required to hug people they don't want to hug.

I'm going to assume that everyone reading this book wants a culture where sexual consent is valued and taken seriously. If that's true, we need to accept that we don't live in that culture. We need to look at our own ideas and feelings about sex, and look at whether they contribute to that culture. We need to speak out when we see consent violated or trivialized, and we need to make it clear that we won't accept it. We need to talk with each other about our shitty cultural ideas about consent, and about our visions for an alternative.

We're atheists. We understand that nobody is going to make the world right for us. God isn't going to do it; the religious right and Islamist theocracies and the Catholic Church are sure as hell not going to do it. We have to do it—and we have to be better at consent than they are. If we want a consent culture, we have to make it ourselves.

CHAPTER FIFTEEN

Why Atheism Needs Social Justice—and How That Might Work

(Content note: sexism, racism, classism, transphobia, ageism, ableism, other isms, dismissal and trivialization of all of the above)

It's no secret that religion can really screw people over. I've written an entire book about that.[1] And it can especially screw people over whose lives are already hard. Religion teaches women that we're second-class and shouldn't have control over our bodies; it teaches LGB people that our sexuality is shameful; it teaches transgender people that their gender identity is an affront to God; it teaches poor people that they'll get rich if they give money to the church; it teaches poor people to accept poverty since they'll get their reward in Heaven; it justifies the caste system in India; it helped justify slavery. I could go on and on. I did.

Religion also provides support, of course, and that can't be ignored. But even this can be a double-edged sword. Many black women, for instance, have talked about relying on support from black churches—who shamed them for being sexual, gave bad medical advice, demanded their unpaid labor while blocking them from positions of power, taught them to be ashamed of having mental illness, and kicked people out for being gay.[2] And atheists of every variety have talked about religion providing emotional and practical support in hard times—which meant they had to choose between lying about their atheism or being left out in the cold. Support isn't so supportive when it asks for dishonesty, subservience, and sacrifice of your health—or when it's the only game in town.

If atheists want to do better than that, we need to work for social justice. We need to create support systems to replace the ones people lose when they leave religion. And we need to work for a world where people aren't in desperate need of these support systems. We need to create a world where people don't step on others so they can feel powerful, and don't push others to the margins so they can feel safe at the center. We need to create a world that *is* a support system, where taking care of each other isn't shunted off to the side, so accidents of birth don't condemn people to a lifetime of struggle. We need to create a world where people can get along okay without religion, and aren't clinging to it for dear life.

A lot of atheists will argue with this. They'll insist that atheism means one thing only—the lack of belief in any gods. In the narrowest, most literal sense, they're right. But conclusions don't stand in a vacuum. They have implications. When we don't believe in God, and we know there's no all-powerful judge to balance the scales and make everything right in the end, the responsibility to create a good, fair world lands on our shoulders. As Terry Pratchett wrote: There is no justice. Just us. And when we understand that there's no afterlife, this mortal life suddenly matters a lot more. There's no God or Heaven—and there are millions of people whose only lives are lived out in misery and despair, for no reason other than the bad luck of how and when and where they were born. That is a fucking tragedy. It is injustice on a gruesomely epic scale. And God isn't going to fix it. We have to do it.

Doing the Smart Thing

If we care about doing the right thing, working for social justice is the right thing to do. If we care about building a strong, visible, effective atheist community that supports nonbelievers and advocates for our rights, it's also the smart thing to do.

It's smart because there are female atheists. African-American-atheists. Hispanic atheists. Working class and blue collar atheists. Transgender atheists. Non-gender-binary atheists. Gay, lesbian, bisexual, pansexual, asexual atheists. Atheists of Asian descent, Middle Eastern descent, Native American descent. Immigrant atheists. Disabled atheists. Atheists with mental illness. Young atheists. Old atheists. All of these folks are atheists, and they all need a voice in how this movement is built. Making organized atheism a welcoming place to all these people and more is the right thing to do—and it's how we're going to turn ourselves into a powerhouse.

And when we fail to do this, we have failed at one of the most central parts of our mission. When women show up at meetups and never come back because creepy men were invasively creeping at them—we have failed at our mission.

When African-American people show up at conferences and don't come back because almost all the speakers were white—we have failed at our mission.

When Hispanic people come to our meetups and don't come back because they got asked, "Are you in this country legally?"—we have failed at our mission.

When people of Asian descent come to our meetups and don't come back because they got told, "You speak the language so well!"—we have failed at our mission.

When people without a college education come to our meetings or online forums and don't come back because they heard patronizing talk about how college-educated people are more likely to be atheists and this means atheism is smarter and better—we have failed at our mission.

When young people get invited to give input to local groups and don't come back because every idea they offered got shot down—we have failed at our mission.

When trans people come to our meetups and don't come back because they were asked invasive questions about the state of their genitals—we have failed at our mission.

When the very idea of having sexual harassment policies at atheist conferences turns into a firestorm of bitter controversy that eats the Internet for months, and when women outside organized atheism hear about this and say, "Screw that, I'm an atheist but I sure as hell don't want to be part of that movement"—we have failed at our mission.

When poor and working-class people don't show up for our meetings and conferences because they're expensive or aren't near public transportation—we have failed at our mission.

When parents don't show up at our meetings or conferences because we don't provide child care and they can't afford a babysitter—we have failed at our mission.

When people with disabilities don't come to our meetings or conferences because they're not accessible—we have failed at our mission.

When deaf people don't come to our meetings or conferences because we don't have sign language interpreters—we have failed at our mission.

When people with mental illness come to our meetings or conferences and don't come back because speakers or members were using the words "crazy," "cuckoo," or "insane" in mocking and derogatory ways—we have failed at our mission.

When African-Americans talk to group organizers about racism and get told, "We don't exclude anyone," as if not barring the door to black people was all anyone needed to do to make their group inclusive—we have failed at our mission.

When women come to online forums and don't come back because they were called bitches and whores and cunts, and the people who complained were told to lighten up and grow a thicker skin—we have failed at our mission.

When marginalized people of all varieties don't participate in our meetings, conferences, blogs, videos, podcasts, forums, chat rooms, and more, because they were all about issues that primarily concern white, middle-class, middle-aged, college-educated, cisgender men—we have failed at our mission. When marginalized people of all varieties point this omission out and ask us to pay more attention to atheist issues that are more relevant to them, and get told organized atheism can't do this because it would be mission drift—we have failed at our mission.

And when marginalized people of all varieties point any or all of this out, and get gaslighted or dismissed or told to stop talking about it—we have failed at our mission. When marginalized people point out ways they felt excluded and get told, "No, you didn't," or, "You're being divisive," or, "You're blowing things out of proportion," or, "We didn't mean to exclude you, therefore you didn't feel excluded, therefore you should stop asking us to change"—we have failed at our mission. When people's basic right to be treated with dignity and equality gets called the five percent we disagree on, and we get asked to shut up about it so we can work on issues that really matter—we have failed at our mission.

All this is stuff that really happens. I have heard of, seen, or experienced every one of these incidents in organized atheism. In some cases, I've seen them again and again and again. There are a hundred thousand ways we show unintentional bias towards marginalized people: there's more than ample research on this, do a Google search on the terms "microaggressions" and "unconscious bias" if you want to see it. That doesn't make us bad people: it means we've unconsciously picked up on the biases of our culture, and that's understandable. But it does mean we have to accept this reality, take responsibility for it, and work to be better. And it means that, since we have unintentional bias, we have to make a conscious effort to overcome it. It's not going to happen any other way. There's no other way for organized atheism to become genuinely inclusive, diverse, and representative of all atheists.

But What about Mission Drift?

If the atheist and skeptical movements focus on social justice, won't that create mission drift?

No.

When we push atheist and skeptic organizations to focus more on social justice, we're not asking them to change their missions. We're asking them to focus on social justice in internal matters, like hiring and event organizing. And we're asking them to expand their appeal to demographics they don't usually attract, by working on social justice in ways that are consistent with their missions.

Let's start with skepticism. The skeptical movement is about rationality, critical thinking skills, evidence-based thinking, and the scientific method. It does education and advocacy about these methods, and uses them to investigate testable questions in the real world, like claims about faith healing. Awesome. Testable claims about social justice get made *all the time*—about gender-role training in infants, racial profiling by cops, children raised in same-sex relationships, unconscious racial biases, the effectiveness of the drug war. I could go on for pages. It's absolutely within our mission to examine these claims and advocate for evidence-based thinking about them. In fact, the skeptical movement already focuses on political and social issues: it exposes global warming denialism and questions the value of organic food. Why is there such fear that social justice will pull skepticism away from its roots?

Now let's look at atheism. The big atheist organizations are working on atheist visibility, creating communities and support systems, opposing anti-atheist bigotry, fighting for our civil rights, fighting for church/state separation, creating philanthropic opportunities for atheists, and opposing the harm done by religion. All this can absolutely be expanded into social justice. We can do atheist visibility programs aimed at African-Americans, women, and other marginalized folks. We can work on making our communities and support systems more welcoming to a wider variety of people. We can look at how anti-atheist bigotry plays out in different communities, and make sure our work targets those communities. We can work on church/state separation issues that are especially important to marginalized people, like abstinence-only sex education or voucher funding for religious schools. We can make sure our philanthropic work targets marginalized people, and listen to what kind of support these folks say they want. We can work on ways religion harms marginalized people, like the religious right's toxic influence on public education.

The atheist movement is already focusing on political and social issues. Many atheist organizations have fought hard for LGBT rights (well, LGB rights, anyway): religious bigotry against queers is one of the most obvious forms of religious harm, and organized atheism has been speaking about it for years. Why is there such fear that social justice will pull atheism away from its roots?

When it comes to internal matters, like organizing events and hiring, this is even more obvious. Of course it isn't mission drift to adopt fair hiring practices; to be equal opportunity employers; to have day care at events; to have student rates for conferences; to have codes of conduct at conferences; to have events near public transportation; to focus on diversity when booking speakers; to make sure events have sign language interpreters and are wheelchair accessible. None of it would change their missions, any more than it would change the missions of the Audubon Society or IBM.

Finally, let's look at local community groups. This is super duper obvious. Local atheist groups do volunteer work and service projects all the time: highway cleanups, blood drives, helping in community gardens, disaster relief. I've never heard anyone complain that this is mission drift. These projects are part of our public face. They're how we change people's minds about us. They're how we push back against bigotry and myths, and show that we're good, caring people with meaning in our lives. They're part of how we let the public know we're here, including other atheists who might not know about our groups. And they're part of how we do our own community building: these projects create social bonds, strengthen communities, and give us a sense of common purpose.

If atheist groups can do highway cleanups and blood drives, we can work on underfunded public schools; racist police and drug policies; abstinence-only sex education; clinic defense at abortion clinics; reinstatement of the Voting Rights Act. Expanding our volunteering into these and other social justice areas might spread our resources thin at first. But it will also swell our ranks. It will get more people involved in organized atheism who aren't right now. That means more resources—more person-power, more money, wider visibility, and a greater ability to do alliance work with other groups.

I'm not dissing highway cleanups and blood drives. These are wonderful things for atheist groups. But when we're looking at volunteer work and service projects, let's expand our ideas of what that means, and start working on projects that marginalized people care more about.

This is the great challenge of organized atheism in the early twenty-first century. And we should learn a lesson from history if we don't want to repeat it. Look at the history of other social change movements: the labor movement, the civil rights movement, the women's movement, the LGBT movement we so often model ourselves on. Every one has been bitten on the ass by this issue. Every one now wishes they'd taken action on it in the early days, before bad habits and self-fulfilling prophecies got set in a deep, hard-to-escape groove. Atheists have a chance to not do that.

Numbers make us stronger—and making the movement more inclusive brings in numbers. Thinking through our ideas makes us stronger—and making the movement more inclusive challenges us to think. And diversity itself makes us stronger. It brings new ideas to the table. It helps us make alliances with other movements. It makes us not look like elitist jackasses.

And atheism doesn't just have something to learn from the world of social justice. We have something to contribute. There's an important place in social justice work for criticism of religion and how it plays into structures of oppression; for more understanding of cognitive biases and critical thinking skills; for better use of evidence-based thinking. And there is an urgent need for social justice groups to be aware of the atheists in their midst, and to learn how to make us more welcome. But we can only contribute to those conversations if we get our house in order.

This is the great challenge for our communities and our movement. Let's get it right.

CHAPTER SIXTEEN

Why "Yes, But" Is the Wrong Response to Misogyny

(Content note: misogyny (obviously), harassment, threats, sexual assault, dismissal of all the above)

Welcome to the world of women explaining feminism. When we talk about sexism and misogyny, in the atheist community and elsewhere, here's some of what we're guaranteed to hear.

"Yes, but not all men are like that. If you're going to talk about misogyny, you have to be extra-clear about that."

"Yes, but misogyny doesn't just happen in the atheist community. It's happening in tech, gaming, comics fandom, science fiction fandom, the world in general. So it's not fair to talk about misogyny in our community, as if it's something special that we're doing wrong."

"Yes, but the atheist community has some great things about it. It's not fair to paint everyone in it with the same brush."

"Yes, but the woman being targeted could have done something to avoid it. She could have stayed anonymous, concealed her gender, dressed differently, not been in that place at that time. I'm not saying it's her fault, but..."

"Yes, but the woman being targeted didn't behave absolutely perfectly in all respects. She did some bad things. Why aren't we talking about that?"

"Yes, but the person writing about the incident didn't behave absolutely perfectly in all respects. They did some bad things. Why aren't we talking about that?"

"Yes, but gender expectations hurt men too. Why aren't we talking about that?"

"Yes, but there are worse problems in the world, starving people in Africa and so on. Why are you complaining about misogyny?"

"Yes, but people are entitled to freedom of speech. How dare you suggest that speech be censored by requesting that online forums be moderated?"

"Yes, but calling attention to misogyny just makes it worse. Don't feed the trolls. You should just ignore it."

"Yes, but what about male circumcision?"

"Yes, but some other feminist said something mean or unfair in a different conversation, weeks or months or years ago. Why aren't we talking about that?"

"Yes, but do you have to be so angry and emotional and over-sensitive about it? That doesn't help your cause."

There is a serious problem of sexism, misogyny, and anti-feminist harassment in the atheist movement. It happens at national conferences, regional conferences, local communities, and online. It includes garden-variety sexist microaggressions, ongoing harassment, threats of rape or death, persistent unwanted sexual attention, sexual assault, and more. And whenever someone points it out, it's almost guaranteed that someone else will respond with, "Yes, but..." So I'm going to spell out why you shouldn't do that.

When the topic of misogyny comes up, and people change the subject, it trivializes misogyny. When men change the subject, it conveys the message that whatever men want to talk about is more important than misogyny. When men change the subject to something that's about them, it conveys the message that men are the ones who really matter, and that any harm done to men is always more important.

And when the topic of misogyny comes up, and people change the subject, it comes across as excusing misogyny. It doesn't matter how many times you say, "Yes, of course, misogyny is terrible." When you follow that up with a "Yes, but…", it comes across as an excuse. In many cases, it *is* an excuse. And it contributes to a culture that excuses misogyny.

So please: when someone points out how misogynistic something is, do not change the subject. Please just say, "That is terrible. That is completely unacceptable. That is not how decent human beings treat one another. Anyone who did that owes her the most groveling apology in their repertoire. That sort of behavior is absolutely not to be tolerated."

Stop there. Do not say "Yes, but…"

If you feel compelled to say something other than "That's terrible," add some thoughts about the history of misogyny; some insights into how misogyny happens and how it gets perpetuated; some ideas about what should be done. But don't say, "Yes, but" and then turn the conversation towards yourself, other men, or some other topic you think is more important.

This guideline applies to lots of conversations, by the way—about race, class, sexual orientation, disability, mental illness, every other form of marginalization. I'm talking specifically about misogyny here, but please do translate: in any conversation about systemic oppression, saying "Yes, but" and changing the subject is almost never a good idea.

If you want to talk about starving people in Africa, circumcision, a possibly mean and unfair thing another feminist said at another time and place, whether moderation of online forums is censorship—fine. Those are worthwhile topics (except for the last, which is just silly). But they're worthwhile topics *for a different conversation.* Do not bring them up every single time the topic of misogyny comes up. It's not all about you.

CHAPTER SEVENTEEN

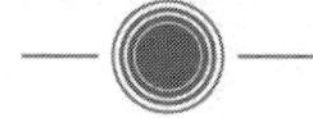

The Part about Black Lives Mattering Where White People Shut Up and Listen

(Content note: racism, dismissal of racism)

Fellow white people, listen up. If we care about racism—among atheists, in atheist organizations, in the world at large—there's something we need to do. It's enormously important. If any other action we take is going to be useful, we need to take this one. And sometimes, it can be really freaking difficult.

We need to shut up and listen.

Black atheists have all sorts of strikes against them. In black communities in the U.S., a huge amount of social support commonly comes from churches, so black atheists have to choose between staying in the closet or losing that support. Religion is deeply ingrained into African American culture and identity, so atheism is commonly seen as a white thing, and black atheists can get treated as not authentically black, trying to be white, even as race traitors. And white-dominated atheist communities can be unwelcoming, even if that's not intended. Pretty much every black atheist I talk with has stories about being talked over by white atheists who want to explain their views on race at great length; hearing white atheists tell them black people are more religious because they're emotional, irrational and uneducated; being told by white atheists that any attention to race is racist and the best way to deal with racism is to ignore it; attending atheist conferences where nobody talks to them. And when they tell organizers about these problems, they're talked over, derailed, patronized, met with excuses and defensiveness and hostility, told the issue is too divisive, or simply ignored.

If we want atheism to welcome everyone, including black atheists, we have to be willing to take action. We have unconscious biases, so we have to consciously unlearn them; our society has deep structural racism, so we have to push against it. And to take effective action, we have to listen.

Listening to the people affected by the problem is the foundation of working on it. When it comes to racism, we have to listen to what black people say: about short-term solutions, long-term solutions, which problems are more important, what the problems even are. "Black lives matter" means, among many other things, that black voices matter. In person and online, with friends and colleagues and in-laws and strangers, wherever there are conversations about racism, white people need to listen.

And listening means *not talking*. It means letting the other person have the floor; letting them decide the topic and set the tone; making sure our own talking is peripheral, done in service of understanding and amplifying. It doesn't mean waiting until the other person stops talking so we can jump in with whatever we were going to say anyway. It doesn't mean making the conversation about us, or holding forth on topics we know little about. It doesn't mean changing the subject to something we're more comfortable with. It doesn't mean telling black people how to talk to us in a way that would make us more comfortable. It doesn't mean telling black people how to run their movement—especially when that advice is almost always to tone it down. It means shutting our mouths and opening our minds.

White people in the U.S. are brought up to expect a lot, often without realizing it.[1,2] And one of the things we expect most is an audience. We expect that when we talk, people will listen; that our ideas will be taken seriously; that any disagreement will be respectful and deferential; that we'll be treated as authoritative even when we're talking out of our asses. We expect that our voices will matter.

But in these conversations about racism, our voices don't matter so much. They're not completely trivial—for one thing, we should be talking with other white people when they're being racist—but they're peripheral. Black people know a lot more about racism than white people. They know more about racist policing and police brutality; about racism in employment, education, fiscal policy, election policy, drug policy, prison policy, urban planning, labor laws; they know more about microaggressions, moments of unconscious racism they encounter dozens of times every day from the day they're conscious until the day they die. Black people, and other people of color, are the experts on racism in a way white people will never be.

And the conversation about racism *is about black people.* It's about black lives and experiences. It's not about us, except in terms of how we affect black people and other people of color. White voices are not the ones that matter.

Here are a few specific ways to listen. We can read books and articles by black authors, and follow black writers and activists on social media. When people on social media link to work by black writers, we can read it—the whole piece, not just the headline. When we're talking about racism, we can share and quote black voices. Atheists in particular can read and follow black atheists.[3] When an unfamiliar concept comes up in a conversation about race, we can Google it.

If a black person says something about race we don't agree with, instead of arguing, we can ask. And when we ask, we can understand how exhausting it can be to do Racism 101 every day for a lifetime, and acknowledge that it's a favor, not an obligation. If the answer is "Here's a nice Racism 101 resource" or even "Do your own damn

Googling," we can accept it. We can understand that our desire to be educated on demand does not take priority over black people's desire to talk about what they want, when they want, and with whom.

We can accept that we have racist ideas, and when someone points one of them out, we can react with something other than "I'm not a racist, how dare you say that!" If we're criticized about racism, we can listen to the content and let go of the tone. We can recognize that our hurt feelings over being told we said something racist are not as important as racism itself. We can think before we respond: we can stop talking, look things up, talk with other people, think some more, and let ourselves cool off. We can consider whether we need to respond at all, with anything other than "Sorry" or even "I'm not sure I agree, but I'm listening, let me think about that." We can quit responding to critiques of racism with "Lighten up," "You're being too sensitive," or "That's so PC." That is literally saying to black people that the things that matter to them don't matter to you, or to anyone—they only matter to black people, and black people don't count.

And whenever this is uncomfortable or upsetting, we can remember that *this is not about us*: that as painful as these conversations might be for us, racism is a thousand times worse. We can remember that white people have been the center of attention for centuries—and we can let these conversations be led by the people they're about.

I get that this can be hard. We're all the center of our own universes, and we all want things to be about us. And atheists especially love dialogue, debate, the free and open examination and questioning of ideas. I love those things, too. But if we care about racism, about making atheist communities and the insides of our heads less racist, we need to care about justice, human rights, ethics, and compassion, more than the sound of our own voices. In these conversations about racism, that means shutting up and listening.

CHAPTER EIGHTEEN

Trans People and Basic Human Respect

(Content note: transphobia and anti-trans violence)

I've been thinking about cisgender people who get upset about transgender people. (Cisgender, if you aren't familiar with the term, is the opposite of transgender: it means someone whose gender identity corresponds with the sex they were assigned at birth.) Some cis people object to trans people's names, pronouns, other changes in language they're asking for. Others object to the very existence of trans people: they think gender is fixed at birth, and that any other perception is just silly.

Here's what's puzzling me: Why do these people care?

It would be awesome if this were never an issue in atheism. Unfortunately, many atheists have terrible ideas about transgender people, conscious and unconscious. They might stem from religion or a hundred other sources, but they still shut trans people out of atheist spaces, and they're still our responsibility. Some of those terrible ideas are based on simplistic, misinformed ideas about biology; some are based on unquestioned, "common sense" preconceptions masquerading as rationality. There's even atheist hostility to trans people based on feminism—outdated second-wave feminism glued so tightly to a specific feminist theory that it shuts out both reality and compassion.[1] I come back to my question: Why do these people care?

Let's assume, purely to disprove it, that trans people are somehow mistaken: that they "really" are the gender they were assigned at birth based on their genitals, and it's silly for them to think otherwise. I obviously don't think that—it's a deeply offensive opinion, out of touch with well-documented reality. But to demonstrate how wrong it is, for the sake of argument let's assume it's true.

So what? How could it possibly affect you? If someone is identifying with a gender you personally think is wrong—how does it harm you in any way?

There are a lot of reasons people care. Accepting the existence of trans people makes everyone else re-think gender, in ways that may be unsettling. If we're invested in the idea that gender roles are completely inborn, it makes us re-think that: if we're invested in the idea that gender is 100% socially constructed, it makes us re-think *that.* It makes us re-think masculinity and femininity, in ways that may undercut our own. It makes us re-think the very idea of a gender binary—the idea that there are only two genders that are distinct and easy to identify. It makes us re-think what gender even is. And accepting the existence of trans people can make cis people re-think our own genders. I get that this can be difficult.

But I still don't have patience with it. If other people's existence make us question our assumptions, is that a bad thing? Atheists and skeptics are supposed to question our assumptions. If our assumptions require us to close our eyes to reality, to ignore not only extensive research but the lived experience of millions, to deny the existence of entire categories of people, we should question them. That's true for people with traditional views of gender, convinced that men are men, women are women, they're easy to distinguish and that's all there is to it. It's true for people with the belief that God made us male and female at birth and we shouldn't question his ways, or who hold the naturalistic fallacy that gender is determined by birth genitals. And it's true for the hateful trans-exclusionary feminists (a small subset of feminists, but an unfortunately vocal one), who reject trans people's very existence because accepting them would undercut the particular feminism they're glued to. When our assumptions lead us to internal contradictions or ethical horrors, they've got to go.

Trans people aren't making anyone else redefine their gender. Knowing that trans people exist might make people think about gender differently, but at the end of the day, we can identify as any gender we're comfortable with. That's the idea. So why is it so hard to accept trans people's existence? In fact, why should that even be up to cis people? Why should that be in our hands?

As for changes in language: yes, trans people often change their names, and some do it more than once. Some identify as male or female, others have blended gender identities, still others aren't on a gender binary. Some want to be referred to as "he" or "she," others prefer new gender-neutral pronouns like "zie" or "hir"; still others prefer the singular "they." There are new words, new names, new ideas about how to use them.

So if you're struggling with the new etiquette, follow the old one. To quote Miss Manners: The polite thing to do has always been to address people as they wish to be addressed.[2] When people get married and change their names, when they get doctorates or other achievements and change their honorifics, when they stop wanting to be called by their childhood nicknames, we usually keep up. Is keeping track of trans people's names and pronouns any harder? Misgendering trans people isn't just a casual bit of poor manners. It reinforces, even if unintentionally, the oppressive weight of a culture that disrespects trans identities and tries to silence them with shame, ridicule, hatred, harassment, discrimination, denial of their very existence, and all too often with violence and death. Is it really an imposition to try to get it right?

And some cisgender people object to the word cisgender on the very basis of self-definition. Even if they understand that it's simply descriptive and not a slur, and that it doesn't imply acceptance of rigid gender norms, they still don't like it. They didn't choose the word, so they don't think they should have to use it. That would be a fair critique, if we'd come up with a word for ourselves. We didn't. We were content to let ourselves be called—what? "Not-transgender"? "Normal"? Nothing at all? We were content to let ourselves be the default, the thing that doesn't need a name because it's just how people are. We were content to let our lack of a name mark trans people as other. So a word got chosen for us, by trans people who needed parallel language that framed different gender experiences as equally valid. Cis people had the chance to choose our language. We blew it. We need to suck it up.

Trans people in the U.S. have nearly double the unemployment rate of the general population. They're nearly four times more likely than the general population to live in extreme poverty. 19% have been refused a home or an apartment, and 11% have been evicted, based on their gender identity. 41% have attempted suicide. And violence against trans people is epidemic. 78% of trans people in the U.S. have been harassed in grade school and high school; 35% were physically assaulted in school; over 50% of have experienced sexual violence at some point in their lives. (Not incidentally, most of these incidents disproportionately involve trans people of color.) And these numbers are probably low: violence against trans people is almost certainly under-reported.[3,4]

Given all this—are cis people really going to complain because we have to re-think our ideas about gender, and have to remember some unfamiliar pronouns?

Trans people exist. If we're rationalists, we should accept that. Trans people are people: if we're humanists, we need to apply that to all humanity. Respecting people's right to define themselves, and acknowledging that they know more about their bodies and lives than we do, is not too much to ask.

CHAPTER NINETEEN

Sex Work and a Catch-22

(Content note: mistreatment of sex workers, including shaming, ignoring, passing mentions of violence)

Whenever I write about sex work, I stumble across a catch-22. It's about my motivations for getting into the business: Did I do it out of economic necessity, for personal pleasure, or some combination of the two?

The catch-22 is this. If I say I became a nude dancer for money, I feed the stereotype of sex workers as victims. I feed the idea that nobody wants to do sex work, it's always unpleasant and often abusive, and nobody does it unless they're coerced or desperate. But if I say I became a nude dancer for pleasure, I get pegged as a dilettante, nothing like the real workers in the trenches. It's a classic No True Scotsman fallacy: enjoying sex work makes me not a real sex worker by definition. And if I didn't feel financial pressure to get into the business, anything I say about it is seen as diminishing people who do it because they have to. Plus, if I say that pleasure was a big reason for getting into the business, I get dismissed as a slut.

The reality is that I was motivated by both economic pressure and sexual pleasure. Sexual curiosity was already sparking my interest in nude dancing, but I didn't do it until I had to pay off a student loan debt (to a Jesuit university, ironically enough). If it hadn't been for that debt, I don't know if I would have mustered my courage and stepped onto that stage. And that's true for a lot of sex workers. Money and sex are both factors: we do sex work for money, but we wouldn't have considered it if we hadn't been adventurous about sex. But there's no way to talk about either motivation without being seen as a desperate victim or a trifling slut.

Religion is famous for slut-shaming and whore-shaming. The idea that our bodies belong to God and not to us, that God and his self-appointed representatives can tell us what to do with them, is entrenched in many religions. But religion isn't the only source of this attitude. Women are told every day, in hundreds of ways, that our bodies belong to men—when men make unsolicited comments on our bodies, or we're blamed for sexual assaults because our clothing supposedly signaled that we were up for grabs. And plenty of secular laws play into the notion that our bodies aren't our own; laws about assisted suicide, drug use, and of course sex work. Even if all these attitudes originated in religion (and I'm not sure they did), they play out in secular ways every day. So secular people need to examine these ideas, expose them—and in most cases, take them out into the street and have them shot.

And that includes our ideas about sex work.

I don't have space here to dissect anti-sex-work attitudes, either from the left or the right. I mostly want to say two things. One is that if we're humanists, our views on sex work have to be rooted in the principle that our bodies belong to us. If we're not injuring other people, what we do with our bodies is nobody else's business: the law has no right to forbid it, and society has no reason to condemn it. If we don't deride and outlaw dance instruction, martial arts instruction, workout training, therapeutic massage, sperm donation, blood and plasma donation, modeling, acting, or any number of other professions where people use direct bodily contact to provide a service, we have to question why we should treat sex work any differently.

The other point is that if we're skeptics, our views on sex work have to be based on good evidence—including the understanding that there's a lot of crappy research on sex work, there's a lot of bad reporting on that research, and the way sex work is depicted in media is usually bullshit. Our views have to be based on good evidence—and that means listening to sex workers. When you do that, you'll find our experiences are hugely varied, with some people who love the work and consider it their calling, others who are forced into it with violence and threats, and many more in between. The sex industry has people who weren't forced into it but felt like they had no choice; people who had other choices but didn't have good ones and got into the work willingly but grudgingly; people who had a fair number of choices and decided sex work was best for now; people who had lots of choices and decided sex work gave them the optimal blend of pleasure and money. And there are plenty of people whose feelings change over time.

We need to listen to all these people. We need to listen to what they say about the policies and attitudes that make their lives better, and the ones that make their lives difficult at best and a misery at worst. I'll give you a hint: almost no current or former sex workers say that deriding or outlawing sex work has helped them in any way. In fact, these laws and attitudes make their lives and work harder, perpetuate the abusive parts of the industry, and make the work harder to leave. We need to listen to sex workers, and when we're writing laws and policies, we need to remember the guideline: "nothing about us without us."

I keep thinking of Natalie Reed's essay, "Catches-22,"[1] which exposes how every marginalized group has one or more catches-22 working against them—ways in which nothing they can possibly do will be right. Women are seen as either sluts or prudes, bimbos or ball-busters. Black people are seen as either lazy criminals or trying to act white. Trans people are seen as either caricatures of gender stereotypes, or not feminine or masculine enough and therefore not really trans. Poor people are seen as either leeching off the system or stealing jobs. Atheists are seen as destroying the support that people get from religion, but our communities are dismissed as just another religion. Repeat as necessary. Reed argues that these sorts of no-win situations are a hallmark of discrimination, "the most direct and immediately recognizable way of knowing that a given group has been predetermined to be in the wrong regardless of what they do."

Catch-22s can reveal a lot. The "lazy criminal/acting white" catch-22 shows that "lazy criminal" is seen as the default for black people. The "slut/prude" catch for women condemns any female sexual agency: we get slammed for taking our sexuality into our own hands, whether we say yes too often or no too often. And this catch-22 about sex workers makes us invisible. It makes it easy to ignore and dismiss what we say about our own experience. It's a neat little self-fulfilling circle: all sex workers are forced into it... and if you weren't, you don't count as a real sex worker and can be ignored... because all sex workers are forced into it. And if economic pressure is part of why you're doing it, either you're not smart enough to find other work, or you're a helpless victim who needs to be rescued.

We need to do better. Atheists love to wag our fingers at religious slut-shaming, about birth control, sex education, sex outside marriage, same-sex relationships, and a whole panoply of sexual causes célèbre championed by that the secular left. If we want to keep doing that, we need to make our sexual ethics consistent, and we need to make them ethical. That means listening to what people say about their own experiences. And it means supporting people in making their own choices about sex—whether they're pro bono or commercial.

CHAPTER TWENTY

The Pros and Cons of Caring about Other People

(Content note: passing mentions of sexual assault, suicide, violent racism, homophobia, and transphobia)

I get that doing the right thing is hard. It's especially hard when it comes to big picture stuff: there's so much that's wrong in the world, working on it can make you feel overwhelmed and helpless, and it's sometimes difficult to even know where to start. It's especially hard when it comes to working with people different from you: the potential to get things wrong is huge, and the learning curve lasts the rest of your life. I want to take a beat here and acknowledge that. I want to be honest about how difficult it can be to care about other people's suffering. And I want to make the case for why it's worth it.

Yes, there are cons. For a start, you get to suffer. When you care about other people's suffering, you suffer too—not as much as they suffer, but you do. You feel a small piece of what it feels like to be homeless, to be sexually assaulted, to be a suicidal gay teenager, to be beaten for being transgender, to have your teenage son shot for the crime of existing while black.

You don't get to go for the big bucks. Unsurprisingly, there's not a lot of money in caring about suffering. Unless you're extraordinarily lucky, the best you'll probably do financially is to be reasonably comfortable. And even if you do get lucky, you'll probably turn around and plow a good chunk of your fortune into alleviating the suffering you care about.

You get to waste a lot of time. You get to spend a lot of time trying to persuade other people that the suffering right in front of their faces is real; that the people who are suffering aren't to blame for it; that working to alleviate it isn't futile. Doing this isn't a waste of time, in the sense that it's often effective. But it's a waste of time in the sense that it's valuable time spent arguing for what should be obvious, instead of doing the damn work.

And when you're persuading people that suffering is real and they should give a damn, you get to feel just a little bit guilty about it. As you pry open other people's eyes, you get to feel just a little bit bad about the suffering you've exposed them to.

You get to feel guilty. You get to worry about whether you're doing it right, whether you should be working on something different, whether you could do better. You get to feel vividly conscious of the ways you contribute to other people's suffering: buying products made by exploited labor, banking with banks that exploit the poor, driving cars that spew greenhouse gases. Every time you don't take action, every time you don't help, every time you don't donate money or volunteer time or hit "Share" or "Retweet" on the fundraising letter, you get to feel bad about it. And every time you do donate or volunteer or spread the word, you get to worry about whether you could have done it better, whether you could have done more.

You get to feel helpless. Once you open yourself up to other people's suffering, you quickly become aware of just how much there is, and how little you personally can do. You get to feel overwhelmed; to be vividly aware that no matter what you do, no matter how much you work and sacrifice, there will still be a massive amount of suffering in the world. As crappy as it is to feel like you could have done something and didn't, I think it's sometimes harder to feel like there's nothing you could have done.

And you never, ever get a break. You never get a vacation; you never get to retire. When you do go on vacation, you think about the lives of the people who clean your hotel rooms and wait on your tables. You leave generous tips, and feel how inadequate that is. It's like the red pill in *The Matrix*: once you've swallowed it, you can't un-swallow. Once you know, really know about other people's suffering, you can't un-know it. You have to feel it—for the rest of your life.

I hope I haven't talked you out of this. Because there are pros, and they're not small.

You get to have a life that matters.

You get to make a difference. You get to have a life that's bigger than you, larger than just your own safety and pleasure. You get to feel powerful, in a good way. You get to feel your life ripple out into the world. You get to feel like part of history. You get to look back on your life and see how the world is better because it contained you.

You get to feel a sense of connection. You get to feel intimately connected with the world. You get to touch people's lives, and now and then you get to hear them tell you how. You get to see other people inspired by the work you're doing, and see them take that inspiration into their own work. You get to be inspired by other people's work, and take that inspiration into your own. You get to feel like a link in a chain, like part of something bigger.

You get an answer to the question, "What is the meaning of my life?"

You get to have less cognitive dissonance. You get to enjoy the pleasures of your life, without that twisting, churning feeling you get in the pit of your stomach when you know you're ignoring something important. Shutting out the reality of other people's suffering means—well, shutting out reality. It means lying to yourself; building a labyrinth of walls inside your head and your heart, a labyrinth of denial and rationalization that leaves calluses and scars. It means living in a bubble, in a gated community that locks you in as surely as it locks the world out. Letting yourself care about suffering means you can let the world in. And you can put your feet up at the end of the day, and know you did something worth doing.

And when you care about suffering and work to do something about it, you get to know some of the best people in the world. You start running into other people who also care and work—and these people are amazing. They are brilliant, imaginative, tough, tender, compassionate (obviously), hilarious. They will help you out of a jam. They will pitch in to work on things you care about, even when they're overextended and have a dozen balls in the air. They will listen, really listen, to what's going on with you. They will show you parts of the world you had no idea existed. They will make your world larger, more complex, more interesting. They will inspire you to be a better person. Sitting around a bar or a cafe or a dining table, with people who passionately care about the same things you do, with people you share a history with, laughing and gossiping and brainstorming and eating take-out and planning the future—there is nothing like it in the world.

It seems like a hard choice. But honestly, it's not.

I don't think I have a choice at this point. I've swallowed the red pill, and I can't un-swallow it; I have this knowledge, and can't un-know it. But if I had the choice, I would make the same one again, without hesitation.

TOUGH STUFF: SICKNESS, SUFFERING, DEATH

CHAPTER TWENTY-ONE

Bad Luck and the Comfort of Reason

In March 2008, I went through a crappy time. I've had worse months—months filled with death, divorce, serious family illness. But in terms of the sheer pointless piling up of badness upon badness upon badness, this was easily in the Top Ten. It wasn't just pneumonia and my cat dying: Ingrid had an injury that sent her to the emergency room (turned out okay, but it was scary); I got a nasty second-degree burn; the pneumonia meant I missed a dance camp I really wanted to go to; my hard drive crashed and I hadn't done a recent backup. It got to the point where it was almost funny—except I lost my sense of humor about a week into it, along with my patience. Of course, you can lose patience all you want with the bad things in your life: it doesn't make a damn bit of difference.

This was the kind of month that would make believers in God wonder why they were being punished. Back when I believed everything happened for a reason and thought the World-Soul arranged the universe around me to teach me lessons, it would have made me rack my brains trying to figure out what the hell that lesson was. But this time, I didn't think any of that—and I'm so glad, I can't even tell you.

Religion is widely defended as a source of comfort in hard times. But this was one of the hardest times in my life—and my rationalist view of my difficulties was more comforting than any religious belief I ever held, or could ever imagine holding.

So from an evidence-based perspective, why do runs of bad luck happen? Some of it is just, well, luck. In any random sequence, pseudopatterns—mini-sequences that look like patterns—will show up. Roll a pair of dice long enough, someday you'll get snake-eyes ten times in a row. Live long enough, someday you'll have a month when your cat dies, your hard drive crashes, and you get pneumonia. It can feel like a pattern with a purpose—but it isn't.

Bad things also lead to other bad things, and can even cascade. If you're stressed, you're probably tired, distracted, even sleep-deprived: so you're more likely to make mistakes, get in accidents, or get sick. If you're upset and distracted because your cat is dying, you might crash into a door and have to go to the emergency room. If you have pneumonia and are hopped up on codeine, you might fall asleep breathing steam and spill boiling water on your chest. And some bad things can make others harder to cope with. Even if you're good at taking the bumps of life in stride, a crappy month can magnify every annoyance into One More Fucking Thing To Deal With. That's even more true for big bumps you have to deal with throughout your life. If you're coping with bigotry and marginalization, more crap is being thrown at you—so more crap will land on you, *and* you'll have a harder time coping with any of it.

This view of suffering may sound like I'm shrugging it off and saying "shit happens." But there is deep comfort in this philosophy. When I had my horrible month, I knew what was happening. I understood it. I wasn't afraid of it. And I didn't feel guilty about it.

I didn't have sleepless nights trying to make sense of it all. I didn't have the shameful, frightened feeling that the dogpile was punishment for some unknown sin. I wasn't trying to figure out what I'd done wrong, what I'd done to deserve this, what lesson was being taught that

I was too dense to learn. I didn't feel like it was my fault, and I didn't take it personally.

I understand that not taking it personally can be hard. If shit happens simply because it does, it can seem both meaningless and out of control. Believing that bad luck is a punishment or a lesson is a way to imbue our suffering with meaning—and it's a way to convince ourselves that we can stop it from happening again.

But when bad things happen, I don't want to make desperate, futile attempts to appease my god. I'd rather have reasonable expectations and wisdom about what I can and cannot change. Given a choice between thinking shit sometimes happens, and thinking I'm a wicked person getting smacked down for reasons I can't understand, I'll take "Shit happens" any day.

CHAPTER TWENTY-TWO

How Humanism Helps with Depression—Except When It Doesn't

I've been diagnosed with clinical depression. I don't feel depressed all the time, but I've had intermittent episodes throughout my adult life. I had a terrible bout starting in October 2012: I'm pulling out of it now, but I'll have to be rigorous about self-care for the rest of my life. And I've been thinking about what it means to be a humanist with depression.

I'm not a doctor, therapist, or health care professional of any kind—I'm just talking about my own experiences. I hate it when people give unsolicited amateur medical advice, so I'm not going to do that. If you have depression, take what you need and leave the rest.

Caveats are in order. Can humanism help with depression?

For the most part, my humanism helps. For one thing, I don't have religious guilt or anger over my depression. I don't think I'm letting down my god by feeling crappy about this wonderful gift of life he's given me. And I don't think my god is letting *me* down. I don't think depression is divine punishment or an obscure lesson, and I'm not racking my brains trying to figure out why I deserve it. I accept that this is a medical condition: I have it because of genetics, early environmental influences, serious life stressors, and other physical causes. I do have self-torments with my depression, vicious circles of guilt and shame over the illness. But religious guilt is not among them. What's more, my humanist celebration of sexuality, and my resistance to religious sexual guilt, helped me prioritize sexual function when I was picking meds—and helped me talk with my doctor about that, bluntly and without shame.

Being an outspoken atheist who's deeply embedded in godless communities also has its advantages. My family and friends are mostly non-believers, and the ones who aren't know better than to load religious guilt trips on me about my depression. And nobody in my life is telling me to pray, align my chakras, or seek any religious treatment for my medical condition. Atheists aren't always perfect about dealing with depression—we have the usual human failings, as well as some special ones of our own. (I'll get to those in a moment). But for the most part, we accept that mental illnesses are illnesses, and we deal with them as such.

And my deeply ingrained habits of skeptical thinking have been essential. I've learned to trust well-documented cause and effect, even when it isn't intuitive—and that helps me pursue well-tested treatments, even when my depressed jerkbrain is telling me they won't do any good. I've learned about cognitive bias and how perceptions can be distorted—and that helps me remember that my depressed brain is not the best judge of reality. I know how to evaluate scientific claims—and that helps me sort through treatments and pick a care program. Even accepting my diagnosis in the first place was made easier by my years-long discipline in accepting reality. And accepting that this is a chronic illness, with lifelong ups and downs, makes it easier to ride out the low points and remember that they'll pass with time.

But valuing honesty and realism means I have to acknowledge this: There are times when humanism doesn't help. There are even times—infrequent, but they happen—when it makes depression harder to handle.

I don't have religious guilt about my depression, but I do sometimes have humanist guilt. Central to my humanist philosophy is the idea that life is short, so I want to live it fully, savor it deeply, and fill it with as much purpose as I can. But when I'm having a bad episode, I can get into a nasty, self-perpetuating loop about what a loser I am, wasting my precious life on morbid self-pity when I'm lucky to be alive at all. Even when I'm healthy, I can get gripped with existential despair, a panicky feeling that any moment not filled with intense, meaningful consciousness is a senseless waste. When I'm having a bad depressive episode, that gets dialed up to eleven. And it feeds back on itself: the more gripped I am with humanist guilt about wasting my life, the more depressed I get—and the more depressed I am, the harder it is to feel anything.

What's more, while atheists don't respond to other people's depression with religious crap, we have our own cultural quirks—and some of these have a lousy effect on our approach to mental illness. A lot of non-believers think that because we've gotten the right answer to one important question ("Are there any gods?"), we're smarter than everyone and are right about everything. We tend to think that because we're well-informed about science, we're in a position to educate everyone we encounter about any bit of science we know even a little about. And our familiarity with scientific language makes our amateur medical advice more persuasive—and thus, more dangerous. All of this can seriously screw up how we handle other people's medical issues—including mental health.

I have been handed some unbelievably arrogant, clueless, insensitive crap from non-believers about my depression. I've gotten a bellyful of unsolicited amateur medical advice: badgering me about how my treatment program is obviously wrong, patronizing me about what a fool I am for thinking my health care providers and closest companions and I might understand my illness better than a random stranger on the Internet. (For the record: Badgering, condescension, and belittling are not good ways to approach people with depression.) And I'm not the only one who's dealt with this.

And finally: Humanism doesn't always help with depression because sometimes, nothing helps. Depression is a tough nut to crack. Treatment isn't simple: for me and many people, it involves medication, therapy, help from family and friends, and an arsenal of self-care techniques including exercise, socializing, meditation, spending time outside, eating well, getting the exact right amount of rest and sleep, doing the exact right amount of work, and more—often when we least feel like it. It involves throwing every mental health care technique against the wall, and hoping one or more sticks. And one of the lousiest things about depression is what a vicious circle it is: some of its ugliest symptoms include the loss of motivation to do the things that alleviate it, not feeling like you deserve care and treatment, pessimism about whether treatment can be effective, and the inability to even recognize the illness for what it is. Depression is treatable, but it can be hard to treat. It's not a philosophical failing. It's an illness. And a humanist philosophy isn't going to treat it, any more than it could treat diabetes or cancer.

Humanism can't treat depression. But it's helping me pursue treatment. It isn't perfect, it's sometimes problematic, but it helps more than it hurts. And for that, I'm grateful.

CHAPTER TWENTY-THREE

Mental Illness and Responsibility

My father died on October 1, 2012. I wrote a nice eulogy shortly afterwards[1], talking about his love of books, his booming laugh, his pleasure in ideas, his hilariously foul mouth, his political passion and willingness to fight for what he believed in, his willingness to make an ass of himself in public, the pride he took in my intelligence, his respect for a good argument, his proud atheism decades before it was cool.

What I didn't say at the time was that my father was an alcoholic—a pretty bad one, and a significantly worse one as the years and decades wore on. Largely due to his alcoholism, he often behaved very badly. He was often selfish, irresponsible, callous, quick with a barbed comment for his own entertainment, dismissive of other people's feelings, and unconcerned with how his actions affected others. I never saw him as abusive, but he could be a real asshole. And it got worse, much worse, as the years went on and the disease of alcoholism progressed.

I don't want to get into the details of his behavior. It's too upsetting, and it's not the point. The point—the question I've spent decades asking myself, as I took step after step away from my father and it kept not being enough—is this: Are people with mental illness, including alcoholics and other drug addicts, responsible for our behavior?

On the one hand: We cut sick people slack. We don't hold them as responsible for their behavior as healthy people. We understand that sick people can't always keep promises or do their share, that they get irritable or lose their temper. We understand it's the illness causing this behavior, and we get angry at the illness, not at them. And mental illnesses—including alcoholism and other drug addictions—are illnesses.

On the other hand: There's a limit to that. We cut sick people slack, but not infinite slack. We'd probably cut a sick person slack for losing their temper and snapping at their spouse—but not for losing their temper and beating their spouse. We would condemn that, and rightly so.

On the other hand: Mental illness is, in some sense, an illness of the will and the self, in a way other illnesses are not, and that's especially true with addiction. So with mental illness, it's harder to distinguish between the illness and the person. The symptoms of cancer or diabetes don't include self-involvement, loss of judgment, poor impulse control, or irresponsibility. And they don't include the inability to recognize that you're ill, take your illness seriously, and get treatment for it. Many mental illnesses, including addiction, have exactly these symptoms. So getting angry at my alcoholic father for having poor judgment is like getting angry at a diabetic for losing a toe.

On the other hand: Some people do recover from addiction. Some people realize they're fucking up their lives and the lives of people they love, and get help. Others don't. So isn't it reasonable to be angry at addicts, and other people with mental illness, when they don't get help?

On the other hand: We don't really know why some people recover from addiction and others don't—any more than we know why some people recover from cancer and others don't. Addiction and other mental illnesses are diseases of the self, and that includes the ability to see that you're sick; to see the effect your illness has on others; to see yourself as worthy of help; and to muster the motivation to do something about it. So getting mad at addicts and other mentally ill people for not working on recovery is like getting mad at someone with HIV for getting opportunistic infections. In fact, we don't understand addiction and other mental illnesses very well at all. Some addicts, and people with other mental illnesses, do seek treatment, and it doesn't always work. It often doesn't work. Sometimes it works for a while and then stops; my father dried up for years, and then started drinking again not long after my mother died. Some treatments work for some people and not others; some of the most popular treatments for addiction don't work any better than people quitting on their own. We don't know why, for any of this. And of course, some people have better access to treatment, better support systems, easier environments to recover in. So a commitment to recovery is no guarantee of getting better.

On the other hand: If my father had made an effort to quit other than that one time, if he'd tried treatment a dozen times and just kept relapsing, I think I wouldn't be as angry as I am. It's common, a cliché even, for alcoholics to deny they're alcoholics. But my father knew he was an alcoholic, acknowledged it openly, even dried up for a while. His denial took a somewhat unusual form: he denied that the alcoholism was a problem. He denied that it was serious, that it was screwing up his life, that it was ruining his health and ability to do things he cared about, that it was hurting and alienating the people closest to him. He knew he was an alcoholic—so doesn't that make him responsible for it? If you can't see you're alcoholic, that's one thing. But if you do see it, and you shrug it off and say, "It's not a big deal, I don't mind and y'all aren't worth the trouble of getting better," doesn't that make you morally culpable?

On the other hand: I've done much the same thing with my depression. My depression is intermittent—so for years, when I was depressed, I used to say, "It's not a big deal. I can manage this. I don't need help." I'm sure those episodes were longer and more severe because

I wasn't getting treatment. And I know I behaved badly during those episodes, worse than I would have if I'd gotten help. Should I be held responsible for that? The denial of the seriousness of a mental illness, the refusal to get care for it, is often one of its symptoms. And the inability to see yourself as deserving of help is also a symptom. Even when you know your illness is harming your relationships, mental illness can make it harder to see your relationships as worth preserving, to see yourself as someone who others rightly value and love. So if an illness blocks your motivation to get help, keeps you from taking it seriously, and even makes you unable to see that you have it—are you responsible for not getting help?

In *Touching a Nerve: The Self as Brain*, in the chapter on Free Will, Habits, and Self-Control, neurophilosopher Patricia S. Churchland points out that self-control depends on physical structures in the brain. She argues that of course we have free will and the ability to choose our behavior—because we have brain structures that let us do that. We're not barnacles or bacteria. "If you are *intending* your action, *knowing* what you are doing, and are of sound mind, and if the decision is not coerced (no gun is pointed at your head)," she argues, "then you are exhibiting free will." And she points out that self-control can be learned—in childhood anyway.[2]

Useful information, and insightful. But it's really just begging the question. Sure, the ability to choose our behavior is part of our brain structure and chemistry. But do we choose our brain structure? Especially if we have mental illness? How much of our brain structure is determined by genetics, in utero environments, early diet, by parents and teachers and whatever crap was in the water we drank when we were three? Of course we choose our brain chemistry in lots of ways: we choose to exercise, spend time in the sunlight, take medication, or we choose to drink heavily, isolate ourselves, stay inside on the sofa all day. And if self-control can be acquired, a case could be made that we have the moral responsibility to acquire it. But if these choices are being made by a brain that's already shaped, by everything that's happened to it so far, to be crappy at making choices—how much responsibility do we have for that?

In fact, Churchland herself points out that the ability to choose is not a simple matter of either/or. She points out that exercising self-control is exhausting—and wonders if some of us exhaust more easily than others. Discussing a colleague, a surgeon with Tourette's Syndrome who can perform surgery without tics but can't restrain them on an everyday basis, she says, "It is not exactly that he is entirely out of control; nor is he fully in control. He is somewhere in between."

If we're all in between—and I think we are—where on that spectrum does responsibility lie?

I keep going back and forth. I've been going back and forth for decades; I've been writing this piece in my head for years. And I realize the answer is not either/or. The answer is that our moral responsibility falls somewhere on a spectrum, somewhere between in control and out of control, and there are big messy gray areas where navigation is difficult and painful. But that's not a very useful answer.

Or maybe it is useful, and accurate—and it's just hard to accept.

CHAPTER TWENTY-FOUR

My Body Is the Knife: The Reality of Medical Uncertainty

If we don't know the answer to a question, the best thing to do is say so. Then, of course, we should investigate and try to find an answer. We shouldn't jump in with an uninformed guess based on our cognitive biases. And we shouldn't assume that because we don't know the answer to a question, that answer must be God. We should let the question be unanswered.

Atheists and skeptics love to say this. It's all very well and good: I totally agree. But what do you do if the question on the table is one you need an answer to? What if the question isn't abstract or distant, like why there's something instead of nothing? What if the question has an immediate, practical, non-trivial impact on your everyday life? Something like, oh, say, just as a random example, "What are my chances of getting cancer, and what should I do to prevent it and detect it early?"

A few years ago, I got a presumptive diagnosis of Lynch Syndrome. This is a genetic syndrome that gives you about an 80% chance of getting colon cancer, a 20%-60% risk of endometrial cancer, and a somewhat increased chance of some other cancers, including an as-yet-unknown-but-possibly-as-high-as-ten-or-twenty percent chance of stomach cancer.

I say I got a presumptive diagnosis: they didn't find the genetic markers that normally point to Lynch Syndrome, but according to the genetic counselor, I almost certainly have it. I've had two Lynch Syndrome cancers: I had a hysterectomy for endometrial cancer in 2012, and my last few colonoscopies found pre-cancerous adenomas which would have turned to cancer if they hadn't been removed. My colon is slowly but constantly growing little cancers. And my family history is pretty much a Lynch Syndrome textbook. It's entirely possible—likely, even—that there are genetic markers associated with Lynch Syndrome that researchers don't know about. So we're proceeding on the assumption that I have it, even though we don't know for sure.

So in addition to my now-annual colonoscopies—oh, joy—we had to decide if I should get stomach endoscopies. But my genetic counselor said there are no agreed-upon medical guidelines on stomach endoscopies for people with Lynch Syndrome. "Talk to a gastroenterologist," they said. So I did—and they said the same thing. No agreed-upon medical guidelines. We'd have to make whatever decision seemed right to us, updating it as new information comes in.

You may be noticing a pattern here. Presumptive diagnosis. As yet unknown. No medical guidelines. It's possible. It's likely. As new information comes in. Whatever decision seems right. Proceed on the assumption, even though we don't know for sure.

This is often the reality of science. Some questions are pretty much settled: we hypothetically might revisit them if heaps of new evidence came in, but for decades or centuries an overwhelming body of evidence has pointed to one answer. (Example: "Does the Earth orbit the Sun?") Some questions have the broad strokes mostly settled, but we're still figuring out many of the finer points. (Example: "What the heck is happening on the subatomic level?") And some questions we're very much in the process of answering: consensus hasn't been reached, data's still coming in, we're making educated guesses based on limited information, and our best guesses are changing yearly and even monthly. To pick an example completely at random: "How do genetic factors influence our likelihood of getting certain cancers—and how do those factors shape prevention, early detection, and treatment?"

Those of us who value science understand this. In fact, we embrace it. We see it not as a weakness, but as a strength. Science isn't a body of knowledge so much as it is a process, a method of gathering knowledge, and the fact that it self-corrects is one of the reasons it's so successful. But some of these questions are not abstract. They're very freaking personal, and some are life or death. And the shifting ground of an unanswered question is different when you're living in the middle of it.

The cutting edge of science is hard to accept when your body is the knife.

And I think this is one of the reasons many people are mistrusting of science, dismissive of it, ready to say, "Oh, what do those scientists know? They keep changing their minds! Last year they told us not to eat carbs, now they're telling us carbs are okay! They can't even make up their own minds—why should we believe anything they say?" On a practical, day-to-day basis, the cutting-edge, not-yet-answered science most people are intensely engaged with, the one most people care deeply about, is medicine. And uncertainty in medicine can be frightening, upsetting, depressing, and even enraging.

The cutting edges of astronomy, botany, quantum physics? Most people aren't even aware of them. Their immediate effects on people's lives don't generally start until the science is fairly settled. Even with computer science, most of us don't touch the technology until it's more or less hammered out. But medicine is different. With medicine, a significant amount of research is done on human beings. A case could be made that *all* medicine is research done on human beings: medical protocols are constantly being updated and refined. And when it comes to terminal illnesses, it would be irresponsible not to at least consider pursuing treatments, even if they're highly uncertain. If the choices are "try something that may nor may not work" or "die"—much of the time, that's a no-brainer. (My wife Ingrid got arrested nine times for demanding, among other things, that the FDA grasp this principle and shorten the research protocols for experimental AIDS drugs.)

In the cutting edge of medical science, human lives are the knife. And that can make people very freaking cranky about medical science.

I understand that. I hate this uncertainty about my Lynch Syndrome: I would much rather just have the bloody diagnosis. I would much rather know for sure that I have this syndrome, instead of having to act on the assumption that I have it even when I don't have proof.

This is frustrating as hell. But here's the thing.

Medical science is the reason we even *know* about Lynch Syndrome. Medical science is the reason I'm getting colonoscopies every year instead of every five years, and am getting my pre-cancerous adenomas scooped out every year. Medical science is the reason we know that the tendency to get some cancers is hereditary: it's the reason that, even before my doctors knew anything about Lynch Syndrome, they were looking at my mom's cancer history, wincing, and then insisting I get colonoscopies early. Medical science is the reason millions of people are getting regular colonoscopies and mammograms, and getting cancers and pre-cancers detected and treated. Medical science is the reason colonoscopies and mammograms even exist.

If we'd known about Lynch Syndrome forty years back, my mom's cancer could have been treated before it ate her up at age forty-five. It's painful to think about that. But I can't be sorry that the current medical science, imperfect as it is, is keeping me alive.

People sometimes talk about finding a cure for cancer, as if cancer were one disease, and we were going to find one cure. I think some people are disappointed this hasn't happened: cancer turns out to be hundreds of diseases, and after all these decades, after millions of dollars and millions of work-hours poured into it, cancer research is still about prevention, early detection, improved treatments, and increased lifespans, much more than it's about a cure.

But the reality is that cancer is a much more survivable disease than it was when I was growing up. More people with cancer are nipping it in the bud. More people with cancer are living longer. More people are getting their cancer fully treated, and are living full lifespans and dying of something else. More people with cancer who can't get it fully treated are living longer and better than they would have fifty years ago, or twenty, or even ten. More people with cancer are getting treatment that isn't excruciating and doesn't completely screw up their lives, or that's somewhat less excruciating and is screwing up their lives a little less. And some people aren't getting cancer at all—because they're eating their fiber, because they quit smoking or never started, because they're getting regular colonoscopies and are getting their pre-cancerous bits cut out. Oncology is an imperfect, inexact science, but it's getting better all the time.

Science is why I'm alive. I'm not going to embrace its results—the messy, uncertain, unpredictable, loaded-with-false-starts, "try a hundred things with no idea if any will pan out" scientific process—and then piss all over it because it isn't perfect. Prevention, early detection, improved treatments, and increased lifespans are not trivial. Millions of people are alive today because of them. I'm one.

CHAPTER TWENTY-FIVE

"Everything Happens for a Reason"

I'm not sure when I started noticing this phrase. I think it was during one of our *Project Runway* marathons. When designers lose a challenge and get kicked off the show, roughly half of them say something along these lines: "Obviously I'm disappointed. But everything happens for a reason."

It drives me up a tree—whether it's framed as conventional theism ("God has a plan") or spiritual-but-not-religious woo ("The universe is trying to teach me something"). It's especially irritating because I used to believe it, and I'm always more irritated with irrational beliefs I used to hold.

In the most literal sense, of course everything happens for a reason. Earthquakes happen because of shifting plates in the earth; I got pneumonia because I got bacteria in my lungs; designers get kicked off *Project Runway* because the judges don't like their designs. But that's not what people mean when they say everything happens for a reason. They mean everything happens for a purpose: earthquakes, illnesses, reality show eliminations, are all part of a plan. It might be God's all-knowing plan or the unconscious will of the World-Soul, but either way it's part of a plan, meant to teach us lessons, point us in new directions, or give us things we need but don't want to accept.

And this idea bugs the crap out of me. It bugs me for the obvious reason: it's mistaken, it's not how the world works. But it also bugs me because it's a passive philosophy, and it gets in the way of learning from our mistakes. If we think every bad thing serves some larger purpose, how will we figure out which ones really were our own fault? How will we learn which parts of life are our responsibility, which parts are other people's, and which are just accidents nobody could control?

I get where this comes from. Our brains have a hard time accepting when we screw up. So if you didn't study, flunked chemistry, and now can't go to med school, you'll feel less foolish if you convince yourself it wasn't meant to be and your true fate is growing marijuana. This trope also helps us save face: we look less foolish when we shift the blame for our mistakes, and incomprehensible gods or fates are always good scapegoats. Saving face can be especially important with unpopular choices: if your family was pushing you to be a doctor, you might not want to tell them that you blew off chemistry because the thought of med school gave you hives—so you blame it on fate. And it can be hard to accept how fragile our lives are, how much they're shaped by chance: when we think the crap in our lives is part of a grand plan, it can give it some meaning, and we can be more optimistic.

I get why people think this way. But it's out of touch with reality, and it gets in our way. Yes, we're wired to see intention even when it's not there—but when we see our lives as shaped by gods or fates, it's harder to see what really went wrong, and that makes it harder to do better in the future. Yes, we're wired to rationalize, we yearn for meaning, we want to save face—but this is a lousy way to do it. There are better ways to rationalize: "I was having a bad day," "I guess you can't please everybody." There are better ways to save face: "This was out of my wheelhouse and I didn't do my best work," "I'm proud of my work and wouldn't have done it differently." And there are better ways to find meaning, including my personal favorite: "I learned a lot from this, and I'm going to be a better person because of it."

"Everything happens for a reason" is a passive philosophy. It sees your life as belonging to someone else. It looks out into the world for clues about what to do, instead of looking at your own ambitions and skills. And it's a way of avoiding responsibility. When you say you weren't meant to go to med school, you don't have to acknowledge that you don't want to go to med school; that you screwed up your chance to go; or that if you do want to go you need to make serious changes.

Back in my own woo days. I often told myself I was meant to do X or not do Y: I was meant to live in San Francisco and work for the lesbian sex magazine *On Our Backs*; I wasn't meant to stay in my first marriage or go to nursing school. It was so easy to interpret my successes and failures, my happy and unhappy accidents, as signs from a benevolent spirit guiding my path. The soul of the universe seemed kinder and more thoughtful than the indifference and absurdity of random chance, and it seemed a thousand times smarter and wiser than me.

But I can't believe it any more. The evidence just doesn't support it. And letting go of that belief has made me both more responsible and more accepting. It's like the atheist version of the serenity prayer. When I let go of thinking everything happens for a reason, it helps me have more courage to change things I can, more serenity to accept things I can't, and more wisdom to know the difference.

CHAPTER TWENTY-SIX

The Problem of Nuance in a Wonderful and Terrible World

"Fundamentalist believers want everything simple. They want their moral choices to be straightforward: they want a clear rulebook that outlines their choices, written by a perfect god. They want the world divided into clear categories, with good people in one box and evil people in another. It's childish. The world isn't like that. And the world shouldn't be. It would be horrible. Why would they even want that?"

Lots of atheists I know say stuff like this. I say it myself. And then I have one of those days when I'm hit with a barrage of difficult, complicated choices, and by the end of the day I'm exhausted with decision fatigue and can't even say what kind of ice cream I want. I have one of those days when someone I thought I knew does something not only appalling but completely out of character, and the ground starts to crack under my feet as I wonder how many other friends are hiding crucial parts of their faces. I have one of those days when the sun shines and our backyard is beautiful, and people on the other side of the world are kidnapping children and selling them into slavery, and people on my side of the world are getting shot for being black, and I don't know how to live in such a wonderful, terrible world. I have one of those days, or weeks, or years, or the world does—and I suddenly have a lot more sympathy for the desire for an either/or world.

I don't agree with it. I'll get to that in a minute. I don't think it's an accurate view of the world, and ultimately I don't think it's a desirable one. But I get why some people yearn for it.

Nuance is hard. Nuance is one of the hardest things to accept, and to manage. Many decisions are messy, with different values conflicting, and without one clear answer. (Do I take a bath every day, which contributes to the drought but alleviates my depression? Do I buy computer equipment made in China, which contributes to appalling labor conditions but lets me do the work I do?) Many moral distinctions aren't hard and fast: they're spectrums, and even good and evil shade into each other imperceptibly. (Where does granting forgiveness shade into being a doormat with no boundaries—and where does demanding justice shade into being an unforgiving hardass?) Trusting people doesn't mean certainty: it means being closer to one end of the trust scale than the other, and no matter how careful you are about who you trust, you have no guarantee it will be rewarded. Absolute safety is impossible: no matter how rich we are, how strong, how healthy, how well-insured, how many gates and guards we put between ourselves and the world, we can never be perfectly protected from harm. (If nothing else, an asteroid could crash into the planet and destroy us all.) And we still have to make decisions and distinctions, and move forward in our lives with some sort of confidence.

And we have draw the lines ourselves. When we draw them wrong, we have to take responsibility. We learn from our experiences as best we can, so we can draw those lines better in the future—but we do this understanding that the parameters constantly change, and with no certainty that we'll get it right.

There are moments when I find this liberating, even exhilarating. I feel like shouting from the rooftops: "I'm free! My life is mine!" And there are moments when I find it exhausting, overwhelming, when the burden of responsibility literally feels like a physical burden, like an enormous boulder pressing down on my shoulders.

It's funny. In Christian mythology, the final blissful reward is permanent choicelessness, where difficult decisions never cross our minds. And the gravest sin anyone committed, the sin so dreadful we're all being punished for it today, is gaining the knowledge of good and evil. Yet free will is considered a gift—so great a gift that God allows terrible evil just to let it flower. It's an incoherent philosophy, but part of me understands its appeal, the yearning for a reprieve from responsibility that somehow, magically, isn't a trap.

But ultimately, I reject it. When we follow someone else's prepackaged rules, we retreat from the world. When we slot everyone into boxes, we don't let ourselves be surprised. The hard, bright walls dividing the world become a prison, closing us off from life. And I want life. I want to touch people, and be touched; I have to trust people for that to happen, and if I get hurt sometimes, so be it. Drawing our own lines makes us who we are, and binds us to the world. The world is wonderful, and terrible—and I want to live in it.

CHAPTER TWENTY-SEVEN

Permanent Struggle

I'm trying to make peace with permanent struggle.

I'm trying to make peace with the idea that, in almost every struggle I care passionately about, I am going to live the rest of my life without winning. The day I die there will still be hatred of women, disgust for queers, contempt for black people, revulsion for trans people, pointless poverty, grotesque inequality, stinking rich people who don't give a damn about any of it as long as they've got theirs. I'm trying to make peace with the idea of survival as victory; the idea of harm reduction; the idea that shoving the world into a slightly better place, even a slightly less shitty and unlivable place, is a form of winning. I'm trying to let go of the entire idea of winning.

I'm obviously doing a lousy job.

I'm trying to make peace with how much of our progress isn't really progress, so much as it is digging our way out of a hole. So much of progress means alleviating suffering, righting inequalities, pushing back against bigotry and hatred and brutality, which should never have been there in the first place. So much of progress isn't building something new: it's building a level foundation. It isn't adding positive numbers: it's struggling to get to zero. I'm okay with the idea of permanent struggle—well, no, obviously I'm not, but I'm beginning to see okay on the horizon. I am profoundly not okay with how much of the struggle is such a fucking waste of time. Of course the work is worth doing: the foundation *is* wildly uneven, there *are* a fuck-ton of holes to dig out of. But we shouldn't have to do it. We wouldn't have to do it if we didn't have a terrible history, and if people weren't terrible so much of the time. I'm trying to make peace with how much we could all build, how high we could all climb, if so many of us weren't digging out of these pointless, poisonous, unnecessary holes—and if so many others weren't digging more holes, digging deeper holes, so they can live high on the pile of dirt and bodies.

I'm trying to make peace with how much time and energy and resources we spend convincing people just to give a damn. The world would be so much better if everyone cared just a little more, maybe five percent more they do. I'm trying to make peace with how few people are willing to do even that.

I'm trying to make peace with the idea that struggle sometimes means working with people I don't like, people I have profoundly serious problems with, people I think are a little despicable. It sometimes means letting go of people I once cared about, people I still care about, people I have a rich history with, people I admired, people I loved. Sometimes it means ugly compromise, and sometimes it means ugly bridge-burning, and I do not have anywhere near enough wisdom to know the difference. So much of this struggle is the struggle with myself to learn the difference, and I will be struggling with it the rest of my life. And I'm trying to make peace with the fact that no matter which choice I make, there will always be people ready to judge me for making the wrong one, for taking a stand when they would have compromised, or for compromising when they would have taken a stand.

I'm trying to make peace with the fact that, no matter how far we push things in the right direction, we will still have to struggle—because there will always be people pushing things back. We gained ground and lost it so many times; so much of our work now is regaining that lost ground; and all my good work could be undone in a generation.

I'm trying to make peace with the fact that there will always be people who benefit from being selfish, heartless, willing to ignore suffering. Whatever structures we build for justice, there will always be people looking for loopholes, ways to game the system to their advantage. And they aren't just cackling villains or the one percent. Human nature is selfish as well as selfless, callous as well as compassionate; we are all scared, self-protective, rationalizing, too willing to say, "Screw you, Jack, I've got mine." So much of our history records the battles between our better natures and our worse ones. The struggle for justice is a struggle against human nature—so it will always need to be fought. Permanently. Forever.

I'm trying to make peace with all the ways I'm part of the problem. My comfort is built on other people's suffering; cheap food, cheap consumer goods, plentiful energy, all at the cost of other people's grotesquely exploited labor, at the cost of pouring garbage into the oceans and the air. For all the dozens of ways that I'm living in holes, clawing my way out and having dirt poured on my head at every turn, there are dozens of ways I won the lottery the day I was born—a lottery that was funded by beating people into the ground and taking their money. No matter how careful I am, there is no way to completely disengage from the systems that benefit me at other people's expense. The only way to never hurt anyone is to never engage with anyone, to be a hermit and forage for nuts and berries. And I'm trying to make peace with the fact that I don't *want* to make peace with this. Causing pain and shrugging it off is exactly the thing I'm struggling against. If I'm going to be the person I want to be, I will always question my compromises, doubt my motives, wonder if I could have done better.

I'm trying to make peace with the idea that, even if we miraculously created a democratic socialist utopia with no poverty, brutality, bigotry, or inequality of opportunity, and even if this utopia miraculously had no terrible people trying to push things backward for their own gain, there would still be suffering. There will always be illness, injury, conflict, fire and flood, earthquake, irretrievable loss, death, grief. And even in the best of lives, there are no happy endings. I made peace a long time ago with the fact that life always ends in death, and death is real and final. I am trying to make peace with one of the things this means—that a human life is always a story with a sad ending.

I don't know if this is hard because I've lived my whole life in the U.S., and so many of my country's stories are about winning and happy endings. I don't know if it's just that human minds are wired to see life as a narrative, a story with a beginning and a middle and an end, and it's hard to see the struggle as a never-ending story, a tale that began centuries before we were born and will continue to be told centuries after we die. I don't know why it's so hard. I'm just trying to make peace with it.

At the 2015 American Atheists convention in Memphis, Anthony Pinn gave a talk on what the atheist movement could learn from hip-hop. As he so often does, he said something that strongly resonated, something I chewed over for months, something I wrote this piece in direct response to. As he put it in an email afterwards: "We do what we can where we can, knowing that oppression is weblike in nature. The proper posture is one of perpetual rebellion against injustice."

The price of liberty is eternal vigilance. The price of justice is permanent struggle.

There is this odd way that permanent struggle brings a degree of peace. Trying to "win" the struggle for justice—trying to navigate by the non-existent light at the end of the tunnel, groping our way toward a non-existent promised land—brings a terrible sense of frustration and failure. Letting go of that impossible dream means we can take satisfaction in our small achievements, in the harm we've reduced. We can be smarter about the struggle, make better decisions about short-term goals versus the big picture. And when we don't win, when we aren't perfect, when we don't see our way or any way, it's not because we aren't good enough. The fact that I'm not winning, that the people I'm fighting alongside are not winning, doesn't mean there's something wrong with us. The reason we're not winning is that winning is impossible—and winning is not the point.

And there's a degree of peace in seeing my work as part of something bigger, a link in a chain. There is peace in being one more descendant of Sisyphus, pushing that rock upward, passing wisdom and experience to the next generation of rock-pushers. There is peace in knowing that without our struggle, the rock would always be at the bottom, grinding people into the ground.

I'm trying to make peace with all of this. I'm beginning—maybe—to see okay on the horizon.

CHAPTER TWENTY-EIGHT

Some Comforting Thoughts about Death, and When They Don't Work

Believers ask us, and we ask of ourselves: How do we deal with death? For many atheists, dealing with death and accepting its permanence is one of the hardest parts of leaving religion. For others, death and grief, especially over ugly or unjust death, is what finally destroyed their belief—or made them start doubting in the first place. Our ideas about death are very different from those of believers—and this can distance us from the believers in our lives, often when we need connection the most.

Death is so important for atheists, I wrote an entire book about it: *Comforting Thoughts About Death That Have Nothing to Do with God.* That book reflects most of my core atheist philosophies on mortality and grief. But I can't stick that entire book into this one—there wouldn't be room for anything else—so I'm summarizing the most important ideas from it here. Take what you need, and leave the rest.

We can create our own meaning of death—just like we create our own meaning of life.

Time, change, and the loss and death that come with them are integral to how we think, how we feel, who we are. We literally can't have consciousness without them.

Being dead will be just like not having been born yet. We didn't exist for billions of years before we were born, and that wasn't painful or scary.

Death is part of physical cause and effect in the universe—so it connects us with the universe. It happens because we, and everyone around us, are part of the natural world, with all its wonders and horrors.

Death is part of physical cause-and-effect in the universe—so while it can feel unfair, it isn't, any more than a star going nova. (Note: This isn't true for human-created death, like murders or preventable illness; it's mostly about natural death, especially death from age.)

Death is part of physical cause-and-effect in the universe—so when someone we love dies, or we're facing our own mortality, we don't have to torture ourselves wondering what we did wrong. We don't have to twist ourselves into guilty contortions trying to figure out why we're being punished, or what lesson we're meant to learn.

Death is a deadline. It's *the* deadline. For those of us who are procrastinators—and most people are—knowing life is temporary can focus our lives, inspire us to treasure people and experiences, and motivate us to do something valuable with the time we have.

Things don't have to be permanent to be valuable and meaningful.

When we accept the inevitability of death, we can make better choices about it; about our wills, advance medical directives, end-of-life care, and so on. Research shows that highly religious people aren't well prepared for death: they're less likely to have end-of-life planning strategies, and are more likely to get aggressive medical care in the last week of their life—medical care that's ultimately pointless and only creates more suffering.[1] Religion copes with death by ignoring it and pretending it isn't real. Atheists don't do that. When we're facing our own death or the deaths of those we love, we can make thoughtful, evidence-based choices consistent with our values.

We don't have to go through this alone. Secular grief support exists. There's an online support network, Grief Beyond Belief, where grieving non-believers share memories, photos, thoughts, feelings, or questions, and give each other support, perspective, empathy, or simply a non-judgmental ear. They also have a resource library with funeral officiants, sample funeral ceremonies, secular grief writing, and more.[2,3]

There are absolutely atheists in foxholes. Most atheists have dealt with death in one form or another. We've faced the illness and death of beloved friends and family members, or dealt with our own life-threatening accidents or illness. And there are plenty of atheists, such as firefighters and soldiers, who face death professionally on a regular basis.

The fact that we die doesn't mean our lives never existed. Think about time as a timeline, and our lives as a piece of it. That piece doesn't disappear just because time moves forward, any more than a city you visit disappears after you leave. Death ends your life, but it doesn't eradicate it.

We are astronomically lucky to be alive at all. The odds against any of us having been born are unimaginably huge. Complaining that our lives are finite is like winning a million dollars in the lottery, and complaining that it wasn't a hundred billion, or indeed all the money in the world.

Death is hard for everyone—including believers. Religious views of death don't eradicate fear and grief about death, any more than atheist ones.

Religious views of death are only comforting if you don't think about them carefully. When you start examining them, they don't make any sense. In fact, religious ideas about death can be profoundly upsetting: many believers are traumatized by the idea of Hell, or the idea that their loved one's death was deliberately caused by God. A philosophy that accepts reality can be much more comforting than one based on wishful thinking—since it doesn't involve cognitive dissonance and the unease of self-deception, and you can actually think about it without shying away.

And finally:

Death is natural. And fear and grief over death are also natural. We don't have to pretend death doesn't suck. Religious believers often feel guilty or conflicted over their grief or their fear of death: they think that if they truly believed in a blissful afterlife where they'll see everyone again, they wouldn't feel so terrible. They deal with guilt and cognitive dissonance, on top of their fear and grief. We don't have to do that. We understand that we're a social species that feels deep attachment to others and grieves when that attachment is cut. We understand that we evolved from hundreds of millions of years of ancestors who really, really did not want to die. We can accept death—and we can also accept that dealing with it is painful. And we can let that be. We can experience our fear and grief, and go through it to the other side.

None of these ideas will eradicate grief, or fear about our own death. Nothing does that—not even religion. Atheist philosophies of death don't mean death will never frighten you, or that grief will never distress you. But they can make the suffering and grief less overwhelming. They can give us hope that the pain will diminish. They can help us forge some meaning out of our fear and grief. They can remind us of what we value in our lives, and help us move forward into that life.

Now, when we talk about ways we can cope with mortality and death without religion, there's this weird, hard reality: Some people aren't going to agree. Not everyone finds the same ideas comforting. In fact, a particular view of death might give great solace to Person A—while Person B finds it hollow or even upsetting. Pretty much everything I've written about death and grief and mortality has gotten someone angry or hurt.

I once posted a link to a piece PZ Myers had written about death. PZ had reviewed my book, *Comforting Thoughts About Death That Have Nothing to Do with God*—and he talked about how, as an evolutionary biologist, he sees death. That view, in short: Dying is an inevitable consequence of being alive and multi-cellular. Death is necessary; life is literally impossible without it.[4]

Commenter ethereal had serious problems with this idea—or, to be more accurate, with presenting this idea as comforting. In her comment[5], she wrote:

> *PZ Myers' post is absolutely terrible where comforting thoughts are concerned. It couldn't have been more terrible if he spontaneously converted to Evangelical Christianity in the middle of writing it. Behind the scientific explanation of death (which might be appreciated in a different context), his post is a giant is-ought fallacy. And it's awful. It can be used to justify anything. Ebola? Shut up you whiners, this is how the disease spreads, this is how it kills people, everything is okay, nothing sad here. Hurricanes? This is how they arise, this is how the human body reacts to blunt trauma, nothing sad here. Terrorism? This is how guns work, this is the result of ballistic trauma, nothing sad here.*

She then went on to tell a heartbreaking story about a friend who was killed by a drunk driver less than a year before—and about some of the appalling reactions she had to deal with from religious believers. She wound up by saying:

> *Too TL;DR? Let's put it in PZ Myers' terms:*
>
> *Vehicular homicide? Bicycle dynamics, internal combustion, effects of alcohol on reaction time, blunt trauma. It's natural, nothing to be sad about, shut up.*

What could anyone say to that, other than, "I'm so sorry for your loss, and for how the people around you dealt with it"?

If I've learned anything from what people say about their grief, it's that people grieve differently. Among other things, we have different reactions to different consolations. That's obviously true with how believers and atheists deal with death—but it's also true for different atheists.

For instance: Many atheists take great comfort in the idea that being dead will be the same as not having been born yet, which wasn't anything to fear or be upset about. For me, this is not comforting at all. I'm not afraid of the state of being dead: I just like being alive, and want the dead people I loved back in my life. I do talk about this idea in my book, since many atheists find it consoling, but it does nothing to touch my own fears. I am, however, comforted by the idea that death is a natural consequence of being alive. I tend to see death as unfair, somehow cheating me or ripping me off: it's irrational, but it's often how I react. Seeing death as a package deal with life helps me accept it.

It's true that this idea doesn't offer comfort in the face of all deaths. If someone died too young, or unnecessarily because of brutality or carelessness, seeing mortality as a package deal with life probably won't help. And if there's a particular kind of death that can be prevented or delayed—Ebola, drunk driving accidents, leukemia, murder—of course we shouldn't just accept it. We should work to stop it. But seeing death as biologically necessary for life does help me cope with some deaths; like my father's death of natural causes, and my own mortality. Different consolations don't just help different people. They help in the face of different kinds of death.

When we're grieving, sometimes any attempt at comfort can seem trivializing, and any consolation that misses the mark can make us feel ignored or misunderstood. I talk about this more in the next chapter: when someone is grieving, we often want to give perspectives and insights to make them feel better, but this can seem like trivializing their grief. At the same time, when we're grieving, we sometimes clutch at anything that might offer relief. When my father died, I was desperate to get home to see my brother: I kept thinking "Get home, get home, you'll feel better when you get home"—and unsurprisingly, getting home and seeing my brother didn't make my grief disappear. This can be frustrating, and if we're offered consolation that doesn't help, it can seem like a broken promise. So while I do a lot of public writing about atheist philosophies in the face of death, that's not what I offer to grieving friends or family, unless they ask for it. I put my philosophies in public so people can find them—but in person, what I usually offer is some version of "I'm so sorry. This sucks. What can I do to help?"

Atheist philosophies of death don't make fear or grief disappear. All they can do is lighten the load. Given what a heavy load mortality and grief can be, that can feel hugely valuable. But I know how intense and overwhelming grief can be, and I wish I could offer more.

CHAPTER TWENTY-NINE

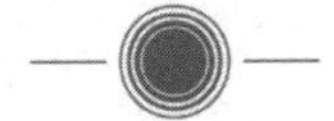

What Do You Say to Grieving Non-Believers?

If you know someone who's grieving, and they don't believe in any god or afterlife—what do you say?

A lot of people, regardless of what they think about God, find themselves at a loss when atheists are grieving. Many social customs dealing with death and grief are rooted in religion: many atheists were brought up with these customs, and when we reject them we often don't know how to replace them. So what, specifically, can people say or do to console grieving non-believers?

There's no one answer that's right for everyone. How you respond to people who are grieving can, and should, vary tremendously with the situation—how close you are to the person, how soon it is after the death they're grieving, their personality, your personality, your relationship. And of course, the right thing to say and do depends on who died, and how. But there are some common words and actions that can help. So in 2012, I took a survey of my blog readers and members of the Grief Beyond Belief online support group, asking atheists what they'd found helpful in their grief.

"I'm so sorry." This is the core of it. Express empathy. Someone is your life is grieving, and you feel bad about it: say so. You don't have to be creative about the wording: grief is a common experience as well as a personal one, and it's okay if your words are common as well. At times when I was grieving, I heard "I'm sorry for your loss" hundreds of times, and I was moved by it every time.

"I remember when... / My life is so much better because of..." In the face of death and grief, we often shy away from discussing the person who died. We think it'll be too painful. But many grieving people say the opposite. They want to hear stories: they want to know that the person they loved will be remembered and missed. This may be even more true for atheists: when you don't believe in an afterlife, the only thing approaching immortality is how people change the world. So tell stories about the person who died. Talk about something sweet they did, something brave, something generous, something funny. Talk about how they touched your life; how much you admired them; how much you'll miss them. (Assuming it's true, of course.) When commenter Dea lost her grandma, the most healing experience was talking with other people about their feelings and memories of how she impacted their lives. "Because that is where the dead live on," she said, "in our hearts, our memories, and if it was family, our genes."

"What can I do to help?" Grief can be exhausting, and it can make it hard to manage everyday tasks. So make an offer of practical help, one that's appropriate for your relationship. When you care about someone and are sorry for their loss, sometimes the best way to show it is vacuuming, babysitting, or making a pot of homemade soup and freezing it into a dozen Tupperwares.

Not everyone will want this help. Some people find routine chores comforting during grief, giving both distraction and a sense of normality. But others will want it and need it. And it's good to make the offer of help as concrete and specific as possible. As Grief Beyond Belief founder Rebecca Hensler points out, "Sometimes, particularly in the first days of grief, answering the question, 'What can I do to help?' can itself be a burden. Offering to do a particular task, for example, 'Can I come by and pick up your laundry?' avoids the moment of panic when the grieving person realizes that she can't even remember what needs to be done, much less do it. Keep in mind as well that a person grieving a spouse is often forced to take on that spouse's responsibilities in the midst of grief. For example, if your grieving friend's wife was the one who always dealt with automobile maintenance, temporarily taking over car-related tasks may be most helpful."

"This sucks." All too often, people trying to comfort the bereaved go overboard with consolations, perspectives, philosophies and insights they hope will make the grief disappear. It's understandable: when someone you care about is in pain, you want to take that pain away. But if someone is grieving, and you keep framing the death as not so terrible, it doesn't help. It can seem like you're trivializing the death and their grief—or like you're trying to make their pain disappear so you don't have to look at it. As katiehartman said, "Don't recite platitudes that are meant to minimize or 'give meaning' to the death. Just don't. Philosophizing can feel shallow, distant, or like an attempt to move on to another topic."

So don't gaslight their grief. Let them grieve already. w_nightshade said that when his best friend lost his father, "he said afterwards that what he wanted to hear more than anything was 'That fucking sucks.'"

Just listen. Jonathan said this beautifully: "I think people obsess about the proper thing to say, when the real issue is figuring out the proper way to listen... All they need to know is that you understand their grief, that you empathize with what they're going through, and that you're willing to shut the hell up long enough to let them express their grief."

So listen. Let them say what they want to say. Ask questions about how they're doing—and listen to the answers, really listen, for as long as they want to talk. As Axxyaan said, "They have a right to feel as awful as they do and if that makes you feel uncomfortable, bear it or leave. Don't give in to the urge to fill up the silence."

Offer company. Grief can be isolating, especially when people lose someone close; a spouse, a child, someone they saw every day or talked with every week. Offers of company can make a huge difference. Depending on the person and your relationship with them, that can mean a sympathetic ear, a shoulder to cry on, meaningful activities, or silly distractions. Helen said it very well: "After 1-2 weeks, start actively inviting the mourning person over for a glass of wine and a chat, or for going together for a swim, or whatever quiet activity you used to do once in a while together (especially if they lost their spouse or someone they were sharing their life with on a daily basis). Don't be offended if they say no because it's too early, and don't insist by saying 'But you have to get back to normal', but keep calling once in a while."

Keep offers of assistance going, even after the initial shock has worn off. In the first days and weeks after a loved one dies, people often get a huge outpouring of support. But the support often dwindles as the weeks and months wear on. Sierra said this very well: "Everyone asked how I was holding up the first week, the first month. A couple of years later, only a few, select people ask me that, and it means a hell of a lot more now than it did then." Alice agreed: "Call or check in on people after the memorial service, and keep doing it over the course of the first year, when all of the 'first snowfall without ___' moments will hit."

So stay in touch and keep offering help. The week after someone dies, a dozen Tupperwares of homemade soup is very good indeed. Three months after someone dies, it's beyond awesome.

Finally, and very importantly:

Let the grieving person grieve in their own way. There isn't a right way to grieve. Some people take some time to intensely process their grief: others plunge into work and other distractions. Some people are somber: others handle their emotions with morbid humor. Some people focus on happy memories: others feel angry about past hurts or disappointed over lost opportunities. Most people say that grief never completely disappears, but some quickly manage the worst of it and move on with their lives: others need more time to return to their routines. Some people feel the loss at anniversaries or birthdays: others barely notice these landmarks, but get upset when a small thing reminds them of their loved one, or when there's a momentous occasion they wish they could share. I don't even remember my mom's birthday—but when Ingrid and I got married, it made me intensely sad that Mom couldn't be there and the two of them would never meet.

None of these is wrong. So take your cues from the grieving person. If they're crying, hold their hand and let them cry. If they seem exhausted and overwhelmed, offer practical help. If they're railing against the injustice of the universe, rail with them. If they're making sick jokes, laugh. And if you're having a hard time reading their cues, ask them what they need. Offer multiple options: do they need a shoulder to cry on, help around the house, someone to take them to a silly movie to get their mind off things? As Sylvia Sybil said, "I've found 'How have you been doing?' to be a good question... It allows the mourner to either segue into discussion of the death and their feelings, or to talk about the less personal activities of their daily lives, as they please."

If you're concerned that someone's grief is triggering serious clinical depression, that's different. That may call for intervention, depending on your relationship. But don't tell them, "Sheesh, it's been three months, six months, a year, why aren't you over it?" Don't say anything even approaching that. There's no reason your timetable should be theirs.

And there's one final point about all this advice: It doesn't just apply to atheists. It works with believers as well.

Many atheists don't know what to say to grieving believers, any more than believers know what to do for atheists. We don't want to lie and spout religious platitudes; but we want to be compassionate with the believers we love, and give them the help they need. But most of this advice is just ordinary human compassion, tempered with common sense and an understanding of human nature, and it can be applied to almost anyone. In fact, many grief counselors say it's not always a good idea to bring up religious beliefs, even with people who do believe in God and Heaven. Even believers can find it trivializing and dismissive when people say "You'll see them again soon enough" or "Everything happens for a reason."

Atheists and believers do have different views of life and death. But we're still the same species, with the same emotions. So if you're wondering what to say to grieving believers—say what you'd say to atheists. If anyone in your life is grieving, let them know you want to help, you're sorry for their loss, and they're not alone.

CHAPTER THIRTY

Dealing with Death in an Unjust World

(Content note: racist slurs; racist, transphobic, and misogynist violence)

When Michael Brown was killed by a cop, and his body was left in the street for over four hours, and a grand jury declined to indict his killer on even the most minor charges, I found myself with very little to say.

There are so many ways to handle death and grief without religion. I've written about them in this book; I've written an entire book about them. But the face of unjust death, what can atheists say and do?

It wasn't just Michael Brown. It was Tarika Wilson and her baby, shot by a SWAT team who meant to arrest her companion. It was Oscar Grant, shot while lying face-down in a BART station. Shelly Frey, whose body was left in a car for eight hours after she was shot by a cop who suspected her friend of shoplifting. Wendell Allen, shot by a cop executing a search warrant for marijuana. Eric Garner, killed in an illegal chokehold by a cop, allegedly for selling loose cigarettes, saying "I can't breathe" eleven times before he died. John Crawford, shot by a cop for holding a pellet gun in a Wal-Mart—a gun Wal-Mart was selling. Kendra James, shot by a cop who'd pulled over the car in which she was a passenger. Kayla Moore, suffocated by cops who'd been called to take her to a medical facility but instead tried to arrest her on someone else's warrant, called her transgender slurs, and didn't administer adequate treatment to save her life. Twelve year old Tamir Rice, shot by cops who said they thought his toy gun was real. Sixty-eight year old Kenneth Chamberlain, shot by a cop responding to his Life Alert necklace going off—a cop who broke down his door and called him a nigger before he fired. Seven year old Aiyana Stanley-Jones, shot by a cop who had raided her apartment and thrown a grenade into it.[1,2]

When these things happened, when hundreds of other deaths like these happened, I had no secular consolations. In the face of unjust death, what can atheists say and do? If the person being mourned was one of the black people killed by police in the United States—one every four days? If they were one of the transgender people murdered around the world—one every two days? If they were one of the women killed by their husbands or boyfriends in the United States—more than four every day? I'm not going to respond by saying death is a natural part of cause and effect, and mortality makes our lives more precious, and religious views of death aren't all that comforting anyway. I can't imagine being that callous. Yes, death is a necessary part of life—but being murdered sure as hell isn't.

When people are grieving, what they generally want to hear is "I'm so sorry." "This sucks." "They were a wonderful person." "How can I help?" But in the face of unjust death, these phrases have very different meanings. "Cancer sucks" means something very different than "Police brutality sucks." (If you don't believe me, try making both statements on Facebook.) "I'm sorry your friend was killed in an accident" means something very different than "I'm sorry your friend was beaten to death for being transgender." "Your grandma was a wonderful person, here's how she touched my life" means something very different than "Tamir Rice was a wonderful person, and the fact that people are criminalizing him and blaming him for his death is an outrage." And when your friend's father has died of a stroke, you might help by bringing food, cleaning the house, holding their hand while they cry. When someone's child has been murdered, and their murder was aided and abetted by a grossly unjust social and political system that's ignoring the murder at best and blaming the victim at worst—you can still bring food and clean the house if it's someone you know. But you can also help by speaking out against the hatred that contributed to the death, and fighting it.

With unjust deaths, the personal becomes political. And that includes the personal statements we make in the face of grief, the statements "I'm so sorry," "This sucks," "They were an amazing person," and, "How can I help?" Expressing compassion about an unjust death, speaking out against it, humanizing the victim, working to stop the injustice—these shouldn't be acts of social defiance, but all too often they are.

I do think there are a handful of secular philosophies that might speak, at least a little, to unjust death. And it's worth talking about those. Many former believers say their faith was deeply upsetting in the face of ugly or unjust death: they contorted themselves into angry, guilty knots trying to figure out why God let this death happen or made it happen, and they were profoundly relieved to let go of the notion that everything happens for a reason. We shouldn't offer our philosophies to grieving people unless they ask—I've talked about that in the last couple of chapters—but we can make them available in the world, so people who need them can find them.

But sometimes the most comforting thing we can do is to not give comfort. We can bring food, donate to charity, hold their hand, say we're sorry for their loss. But in the face of unjust death, one of the most comforting things we can say is, "This should not have happened. There is nothing anyone can say or do that will make it okay. It is not okay, and it should not be okay. What can I do to help keep it from ever happening again?"

CHAPTER THIRTY-ONE

Atheist Funerals

What kind of funerals and memorials can atheists have? If many of our survivors are religious, is it okay for them to have a religious service for us, or is it important that our funerals be secular? Should we plan our funerals at all? Should we even care?

Back in my woo days, when I believed I had a soul that would survive my death, I used to say I didn't care about my funeral. After all, I wouldn't be around for it. Then it occurred to me: I am exactly the kind of person who would stick around to see what my funeral was like. I'm nosy and a glutton for praise—if there were a life after death, I would totally lurk at my funeral. But I'm an atheist now, and a naturalist. I accept that the physical world is all there is, and there's no life after death except our memories, ideas, or genes being passed on. And now I actually do care about my funeral. It's the last thing I'll do, and I want it to express who I am.

I agree that funerals and memorials are for the survivors. So please don't send angry emails about how it makes no sense for atheists to care about their funerals, and survivors should do whatever they want. Here's the thing: when people are planning funerals, having guidelines can help. It gives survivors a place to start planning, instead of a blank page to squabble over. And it gives them a feeling of honoring their loved one, and honoring the final social contract with them.

Whether those instructions are detailed or just a couple of broad strokes, they can still help. When my staunchly atheist father died, all we knew was that he wanted his ashes scattered at the Clarence Darrow Bridge near the Museum of Science and Industry, in Chicago near where he lived and died. This gave his family the freedom to create a ceremony that was meaningful and practical for us, while also giving us the sense of honoring who he was. But broad or detailed instructions can both work: my dad was a freewheeling guy and his unspecific guidelines felt very much like him, but if he'd been a detail-oriented control freak with three pages of instructions about location and music and readings and food, honoring those would have felt like honoring him as well. Even if your guidelines are that you don't care about your funeral or don't want any ceremony when you die, it's a good idea to let people know that: it tells your survivors they truly can do anything they want, or that they shouldn't do anything at all.

Of course, guidelines are no guarantee against squabbling. Many people have horror stories of people making clearly stated wishes about their funerals, only to have them ignored or even violated. In particular, many atheists have horror stories about loved ones giving clear instructions for a secular memorial, only to have religious family take control and soak the service in religion. And yes, these are horror stories. Funerals are indeed for the survivors—and it can be deeply traumatic to attend a service that has nothing to do with the dead person's life or values, and is even a violation of them.

Should we insist on secular funerals, then? If we have religious families, and a religious funeral would comfort them, should we care? And if we think a secular funeral is important—whether we're planning someone else's or our own—how hard should we fight?

I'm lucky. My family are all godless heathens, so I don't have to worry about them pushing for a religious funeral or being offended by the one I want. But if that weren't true, I think I'd still hold out for an atheist funeral. One of the biggest charges leveled against atheists is that we don't offer any consolation in the face of death. For me, it's important to show that this isn't true. My funeral will be the last thing I do: I want my parting thoughts to be that an atheist's life, and death, can be rich and meaningful.

But again, I'm lucky. I won't have to fight a religious family over this, and I know how upsetting those fights can be: death and grief can bring out the best in people, but they can also bring out the worst. And I can't tell you what to do about this when I don't know your family members and friends, their beliefs, how passionate those beliefs are, whether there's consensus about religion or major conflict. I don't know where your own balance is between standing firm and compromising, or how much you even care about this. So I'm not going to tell you whether to push for a secular funeral. My only suggestion is that you start thinking about this now, and start talking about it with the people in your life. I keep remembering the storyline from *Mad Men*, when (spoiler alert) Betty Draper's father wanted to go over his post-death plans and she furiously resisted—but when he died, almost the first thing she did was find the instructions he'd left. These conversations are difficult, but they can make a real difference.

It might help to distinguish between an atheist funeral and a secular one. At my atheist funeral, I bloody well want people to talk about how there is no god or afterlife and how life is sweet and meaningful without them—but I'm a professional atheist, of course that's what I want. You could have a secular funeral that doesn't mention religion *or* atheism. You could have a funeral that just talks about the person who died, with funny and touching stories, music and poems and readings, pictures and memorabilia, people sharing how their lives are different because of the person who died. And I'm going to throw an idea out there: when the dead person's beliefs are different from their family's, or when many survivors are religious and many aren't, you could consider having two memorials. If the believers will be upset by a secular funeral, and the secularists will be upset by a religious one, it might make more sense to let everyone mourn in the way that helps them the most.

Here are some of my own plans: maybe they'll help you figure out yours. Ingrid and I want to be buried together. I want some sort of headstone or marker: I'm egoistic, and I'd like a place where friends and family can visit and think about us. We're also leaning strongly toward a green burial. There are cemeteries that act as nature preserves, with unembalmed bodies as fertilizer: it's an alternative to the water-sucking, fertilizer-hungry, chemically-dependent golf courses that serve as modern cemeteries. I like the idea of our bodies making plants grow, and helping keep some land set aside for nature. And I've visited many a cemetery and wondered about the lives of the people buried there—and I'd like for people to do that with us. A hundred years from now, I'd like there to be a place where college students can picnic, where goth lovers can have sex, where travelers can ponder life and mortality, and they can all wonder who Greta Christina and Ingrid Nelson were. I'm not sure what I want on my marker, though—probably something pithy and quotable I said. I should probably finalize that.

I'd like a ceremony in a public place that has some meaning for me. A bookstore; the Humanist Hall where the queer contra dance used to happen; the Center for Sex and Culture; Borderlands Cafe; the Castro Theater. Not a church—not even a Unitarian one. I might even want two ceremonies; a public one for people who cared about my work, and a private one for my close friends and family. I want somebody to read some of my atheist writing about death, probably something from *Comforting Thoughts About Death That Have Nothing To Do With God*. And I don't want my funeral to be that cliché of celebrating a life, not mourning a death. Fuck that noise. Mourning is important, and when people I care about die, I don't feel like celebrating. Of course I want people to say how awesome my life was, and I'm fine with the bittersweet feelings of happy memories and humor mingled with grief and loss. But a funeral should be one place you're allowed to be publicly sad, and share your sadness with others. I hereby give people permission to cry at my funeral.

That's what I want. What do you want? You don't have to care what a Catholic funeral has to be, or a Jewish one, or a Muslim or Mormon or Zoroastrian one. You can if you want to, if those traditions mean something to you, but you don't have to. You can craft a ceremony that gives comfort to the people who survive you, and gives them a structure to comfort one another. Life is a story with a sad ending, but you can write an ending to your life that's personal, memorable, and true.

CHAPTER THIRTY-TWO

Atheism in a Shitstorm

"There are no atheists in foxholes." I'm sure you've heard this, more times than you care to remember. You've heard believers dismiss secular philosophies as shallow, breezy, and hedonistic, blowing away in the face of trauma, mortality, and grief.

It's malarkey. You probably know plenty of atheists who have been through terrible hardships without turning to religion. Chances are you've been through hardships yourself, with your godlessness intact. You may even know—or indeed be—an atheist in a literal foxhole: not the metaphorical kind, but the military kind where they're trying to blow you up.

I want to talk about one of those metaphorical foxholes. And I want to talk about how, in the depths of it, my atheism and humanism not only endured, but helped carry me through.

In October of 2012, I got hit with a serious one-two punch. My father died early in the month; less than two weeks later, I was diagnosed with uterine cancer.

Short of an actual military foxhole, this has got to be one of the most foxholey foxholes there is. If I saw this story in a movie, I wouldn't believe it. It's so heavy-handed and manipulative: who the hell gets diagnosed with cancer two weeks after their father dies? That doesn't happen to anyone. Except it happened to me.

The cancer was treatable, and we treated it. I got lucky (if any kind of cancer can be lucky): it was slow-growing, we caught it early, and it's been entirely treated with hysterectomy. But it was terrifying. Recovery from the surgery was slow, painful, and exhausting. And it was much more traumatic coming so soon after my father's death. I was barely beginning to recover from that shock and wrestle with my grief when the news from my doctor came. Each of these traumas left me weakened, and less able to cope with the other. And of course, the two traumas are closely intertwined. The harsh realities of mortality and grief were in my face every day, for months.

If there were ever a time when suffering, grief, and a stark reminder of my own mortality could have made me turn to religion, this was it. For days and weeks, I kept waiting for that. I didn't seriously think I would turn to religious belief—I know the arguments against it too well. But I kept waiting for the moment when I *wished* I believed, when I thought to myself, "Goddammit, atheism sucks. If only I believed in God or an afterlife, this would be so much easier." I kept waiting for that shoe to drop—and it kept not happening. The opposite happened. The thought of religion made me queasy—and my humanism was a profound comfort.

Honestly? If I'd believed in a god who made that shit happen on purpose, I wouldn't have been comforted. I'd have wanted to find the biggest ladder I could, climb into Heaven, and punch the guy. That, or I'd have been wracked with guilt and confusion trying to figure out what I'd done to deserve it, or what lesson I was supposed to be learning. If I'd had a relationship with an imaginary personal creator who supposedly loved me and yet made that horror show happen on purpose, that would have been about the most toxic, fucked-up relationship I could imagine. When I picture that relationship, what

I feel is rage, guilt, confusion, and a poisonous mess of cognitive dissonance.

But it was tremendously comforting to see this horror show as physical cause and effect. My father didn't die, and I didn't get cancer, because some asshole in the sky was pulling the strings. My father died, and I got cancer, because of cause and effect in the natural world. And the unbelievably shitty timing? Physical cause and effect works like that sometimes. You roll a pair of dice long enough, chances are that at some point you're going to get snake-eyes. You live a long enough life, chances are that at some point you're going to get two or three horribly crappy things happening at once.

That can be hard to accept. It can be hard to accept that we often have little or no control over what happens to us. But when I look at the idea that sometimes life sucks and I have to deal with it as best I can, and compare it with the idea that an immensely powerful being is fucking with me on purpose and won't tell me why, I find the first idea far more comforting. When this shitstorm happened, I didn't have to torture myself with guilt over how I must have angered my god or screwed up my karma, with that guilt piling onto the trauma of illness and grief. And would the glib cliché that everything happens for a reason really have given this shitstorm more meaning? Would it really have been more comforting to twist my brain into absurd contortions trying to figure out what God was trying to teach me, and why the lesson was both so brutally enforced and so obscure?

Of course I can learn lessons from all this. I've already learned lessons from it, and I continue to. There's no way I could be the same person after this shitstorm than I was before it. But *I* get to decide what lessons I learn from it. *I* get to infuse it with meaning. And that's the power I have. I don't have the pretend power that if I pray hard enough and do the right rituals to appease my imaginary friend, my life will always be awesome. What I do have is the real power to learn from the experiences that life hands me, and to use what I've learned to become a better person and make life better for others.

And the secular philosophies I've been writing and reading and contemplating for years have been a tremendous comfort. None of them made the trauma or grief disappear—any more than prayer or belief in God make trauma or grief disappear. But they staved off despair. They gave me a bridge over the chasm. When the worst of the fear and grief felt like they would overwhelm me, these outlooks gave me hope: a sense that life was worth returning to, worth fighting for. And as I continue to wrestle with all this, to move forward and figure out my new normal and find ways to incorporate the Armageddon of 2012 into my life, my secular philosophies are the foundation I build on, and the fertile soil to plant my new seeds.

When I first became an atheist, I wasn't familiar with any of these ideas. I didn't even know that atheist or humanist communities existed. So I had to reinvent the wheel. I had to grind my own way to my godless views of life and death. And I had to go through my earliest experiences of godless hard times on my own. As a result, those hard times were much harder than they had to be. I don't want anyone else to go through that. As terrible as the shitstorm of 2012 was, as much as it continues to ripple into my life, it was made far, far easier by the ideas I learned, the skills I acquired, and the connections and friendships I formed, from my years in the humanist and atheist and skeptical communities.

So let's talk about this. Comfort in the face of trauma is too important—let's not concede that ground to religion. Let's talk about the worst of times, and how our secular ways of life can help get us through. So many people are questioning their faith or have let it go. When they're facing hard times, let's give them a helping hand across the chasm, and a home on the other side.

PLAYING WELL WITH OTHERS: BELIEVERS AND OTHER ATHEISTS

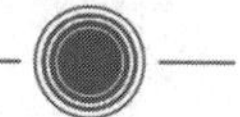

CHAPTER THIRTY-THREE

What Would Happen If We All Came Out?

What would happen if every atheist, every humanist, every agnostic, every freethinker, every nonbeliever of every stripe, went public about the fact that we don't believe in God?

I know that's a wildly ambitious goal. I know it's an unrealistic goal: many people can't be completely open about their nonbelief without risking their jobs, homes, support systems, children, in some cases their safety. So let's dial it back a notch. What would happen if every nonbeliever told one person—just one—that we don't believe in God?

What would happen if those of us who are mostly closeted came out to one person—our mother, our brother, our best friend? What if those who've told some people came out to just one more person—our cousin, co-worker, neighbor? What if those who are already pretty open with our nonbelief came out to our bank manager, our favorite barista, the person sitting next to us at the airport?

This isn't an idle question. I've written a book about this, *Coming Out Atheist: How to Do It, How to Help Each Other, and Why*, a nuts-and-bolts guide to telling people you don't believe in God based on over 400 coming-out stories. It's got strategies for coming out to family, friends, co-workers, spouses; for coming out in conservative or progressive communities, in the U.S. military, on the Internet; for students and parents and people who are dealing with marginalizations. It has an entire section on how to help other atheists come out. And a huge part of the reason I wrote it is that I can't stop thinking about how powerful it would be if every one of us took just one step out of the atheist closet.

I think it would be transformative. It would change the international conversation about atheism and religion, and it would transform our own lives. It would put a serious dent in the bigotry we face and the myths people have about us: when people know us, it's harder to hate or fear us. It would put a dent in religious belief itself: when you ask atheists why they left religion, many say that meeting atheists or hearing about us was a big part of the process. It would help us find each other, and that makes activism and community-building possible. And in the overwhelming majority of coming-out stories I read, people said they were happier after they'd done it. Even when it had been a rough road—even when they'd been met with tears and recriminations, fear and hostility, bigotry and even ostracism—they felt better afterward, and thought it was the right choice. I read exactly one coming-out story from an atheist who regretted it.

If you're in any doubt about the power of coming out, look at the history of the LGBT community. When I was born, LGBT people were being locked in mental institutions. Today, institutions answer to us. And we began to make those changes—in the institutions of law, medicine, the economy, academia, marriage—when we started to come out. It was hard, especially in the early days, when laws and media and hearts and minds were even harder on us than they are now. But each time a queer person told someone, "I'm queer," it chipped away at that hatred and fear and ignorance. And each time an atheist tells someone, "I'm an atheist," it's doing the same thing.

I get that it's hard. I'm not asking anyone to do anything that would seriously screw up their lives. If coming out as an atheist would mean risking your job, your home, your support system, your children, your safety, I'm not going to ask you to do it. But for those of us who can, coming out about our atheism is one of the most powerful actions we can take. It's personally powerful. It's politically powerful. And coming out is what's going to make the world safer for other atheists—the ones who really can't come out without it being disastrous. It could change the world.

CHAPTER THIRTY-FOUR

How Confrontation Can Open Doors

I was in a cafe, paying for my coffee. I'd just gotten a twenty from the ATM. I crossed "In God We Trust" off the bill, like I often do.

The woman behind the counter gave me a look. Irritated, offended. She looked like she wanted to tell me off, or start an argument. Instead she shrugged, and said (paraphrasing here), "Whatever floats your boat."

I felt uncomfortable. Like most people, I don't like upsetting people or making them mad at me. I'm fairly comfortable with confrontation online—it's my job, and it's a job I enjoy—but in person, it makes me anxious and self-conscious. While the woman was getting my coffee, I had a brief argument with myself: was this bit of visibility for secularism worth the offense I'd caused? Had I turned someone off to the ideas I was trying to convey? Was it obnoxious to do my little secular government visibility action right in front of the barista, who was professionally required to be polite and didn't have the option of telling me to piss off? In doing my visibility shtick and trying to open some eyes to some new ideas and questions, had I instead just closed a door?

But here's what happened next. The woman came back with my coffee, and said, "If you don't mind my asking—why do you do that?"

And the door opened.

"Because it shouldn't be on the money," I said. "Because whether or not you believe in God, the government shouldn't be taking sides on the issue. Because I don't believe in God, and if you do that's totally your right—and I want religious freedom for both of us. The government shouldn't be telling either of us what to think about it."

And she thought about it for a moment, nodded, and said, "Yeah, I guess I can see that."

Atheists argue a lot about how to talk with believers: how to do it, when, in what tone of voice. And when we talk about confrontation versus diplomacy, we often assume the two are mutually exclusive. Even those of us who think both methods of activism are useful, and that both used together are more effective than either one alone, often assume you can't do both at once. We assume that you can get in people's faces, or you can have a friendly conversation—but you can't do both.

But this ended up being a civil conversation. A friendly one, even. It was a conversation where I got my idea across; a somewhat important idea about secular government and separation of church and state. It was a conversation where I got someone to think differently, maybe even to change her mind—and it started as a confrontation. In fact, I'll go further. We wouldn't have had that friendly conversation, and I wouldn't have gotten that idea across, if I hadn't been willing to start a confrontation.

And when we're debating the value of confrontation versus diplomacy and accommodationism, it's important to remember: Diplomacy and accommodationism are not the same thing. We often use those words interchangeably, but these are significantly different strategies, and we need to make the distinction.

Diplomacy means trying to get along with people we disagree with: negotiating, working out differences, reaching compromises, finding common ground. It does not mean we never express disagreement.

Ask any professional diplomat if their job requires that, and they'll laugh you out of the building. (Actually, they probably won't—they're diplomats—but they'll use polite, respectful language to express strong disagreement with your position.) We can argue that religion isn't true, and oppose the harm it causes, while being diplomatic about it. And we can be diplomatic while making atheists and atheism our priority.

Accommodationism, on the other hand, means making the other guys the priority. It's right there in the word "accommodate": it means adapting to the other guys, catering to them, working around them, giving them the space. Diplomacy means working with believers as equals. Accommodation means bending to religion as its subordinate.

Diplomacy is working with believers on common ground, from church/state separation to rebuilding homes in New Orleans. Accommodationism is demanding that other atheists never speak against religion because it makes this alliance work harder.

Diplomacy is debating religion in a polite, friendly manner that shows respect for the other person. It's acknowledging when we make mistakes or don't know something; being cautious about which arguments to have in the first place; and being willing to drop it if it becomes too heated. Accommodationism is accepting religion's self-positioning as a special category of ideas that should never be criticized—and pressuring other atheists to go along with this.

Diplomacy is sending a polite letter to the Muslim student association on your campus, letting them know you'll be chalking stick figures of Muhammad to protest threats against cartoonists; saying you understand their distress about this and explaining why you're doing it; and expressing hope for further conversation.[1] Accommodationism is declining to draw Muhammad, and pressuring other atheists not to, because the Muslim faith forbids it and you think we should accommodate that faith.

Diplomacy is a science advocacy organization saying they defend freedom of religion and encourage both believers and non-believers to join, even though science and religion are fundamentally different approaches to truth claims. Accommodationism is a science advocacy organization saying science and religion don't conflict in any way.

Diplomacy is pushing back against atheist critiques of religion when they're inaccurate, unfair, poorly-aimed, or disproportionate. Accommodationism is trying to stop atheists from ever criticizing religion, because you think it's inherently disrespectful and bigoted.

Diplomacy is caring about believers' feelings as well as atheists', and paying attention to them when crafting your strategies. Accommodationism is prioritizing believers' feelings when crafting your strategies—to the point where you ignore the trauma many atheists experienced with religion, try to silence atheists who speak about that trauma, and pressure atheists into doing alliance work they don't want to do.

Do you see the distinction?

Most firebrands I know—and I know a lot, being one myself—have no problem with atheists being friendly with believers. Most of us *are* friendly with believers, at many times in our lives: we're diplomatic or confrontational depending on context, topic, who we're talking with, and what mood we're in that day. The "firebrand versus diplomat" thing is a false dichotomy: it's really more of a spectrum. And even atheists on the fiery end of that spectrum mostly have no problem with diplomacy. Most of us support and encourage the more diplomatic atheists, and understand that our movement is stronger with them in it. We disagree about some specifics, but we know they're doing something important, and we're glad they're doing it.

The unfortunate reality, though, is that all atheist ideas are confrontational. Our very existence is confrontational. Our mildest billboard and bus ad campaigns, the ones saying "You can be good without God" or "Don't believe in God? You're not alone" or simply "Atheists," are met with outrage, hatred, even censorship. For a lot of believers, our ideas are new, and new ideas are often hard to hear. Our ideas challenge core assumptions people have built lives and families and communities around. And there's a reality we don't always like to admit: When we come out as godless, we're telling believers they're wrong. We are being confrontational, simply by existing. Of course, when people say they believe in God, they're telling us we're wrong too: it's a confrontation either way.

And confrontation doesn't have to be the end of a connection. It can be the beginning of one. Confrontation is often a spark to changing our minds. Ask any good-sized group of atheists how many used to be believers. And then ask how many of them changed their minds, at least in part, because of arguments they read, heard, saw on YouTube, or had with family or friends. I can almost guarantee the number will be high.

I'm not writing this to persuade you to cross "In God We Trust" off the money at cafe counters. We all pursue visibility and activism in our own way, and I'm more than fine with that. I'm saying this: If I hadn't been willing to be a little confrontational with that barista, we would never have had the conversation about why "In God We Trust" on the money is bad for everyone. That was a conversation worth having.

CHAPTER THIRTY-FIVE

Atheists in the Pride Parade: Churlishness and Integrity

How can atheists be civil and friendly with believers, while maintaining integrity about our atheism?

A few years back, I marched for the first time with the atheist contingent in the San Francisco LGBT Pride Parade. It was an awesomely fun day, even with hanging around for over three hours waiting our turn to get into the parade. We had a good fifty people: it was a fun and marvelously motley crew, and marching with them was a blast. And we got lots of love and support from the crowd, from generic "Woo-hoo!"-ing to intense outpourings of emotion. (We also got a certain amount of blank, deer-in-the-headlights stares, and the occasional bit of pushback—but mostly, we got love and support.) It was very gratifying, and more fun than a barrel of narwhals.

But because contingents are mostly organized by theme, we wound up marching behind assorted LGBT religious groups: the Metropolitan Community Church; the gay Catholic organization Dignity; the gay evangelical group whose name I don't remember, the ones who had the float with the giant rainbow cross. So the three-plus hours waiting to get into the parade was spent in fairly close quarters with these religious groups.

This posed an all-too-familiar conundrum. How can I be civil and friendly with believers—not just believers I'm hanging out with watching the Giants game, but believers who are actively representing their religion—while maintaining my atheist integrity? My basic principle is to treat people with respect and dignity, while retaining the right to criticize and even insult ideas. That's pretty straightforward in theory. But how does it play out in practice?

I'm going to be clear: I'm speaking here only for myself. I'm not speaking for any organizations hosting the atheist contingent in the Pride parade, or for any other participants. These ideas are my own.

Here was the situation. Many people in the religious contingents wanted to be friendly and make nice with the atheists. Many smiled and gave us the thumbs-up; many cheered and applauded us. Some even made more overt gestures: when we were hanging about waiting our turn to march, one woman from the queer evangelical group came over to chat about David Byers' sign, "Leviticus Says... Crazy Shit." She told us how much she agreed with it, and how those bad homophobic rightwingers were bolloxing up God's true message, and how in the end it was really all about love.

Nice, right? Here's the problem.

In the last several years, I've had many conversations with progressive interfaith believers. In my experience, their tolerance for atheists dries up fast as soon as we start discussing atheism. They tell us that God's true message is love, and we reply that God's true message is that he doesn't exist. They find out that we don't agree with any religion, that we're familiar with progressive religion and still don't believe. They find out that for many of us, our attitude toward progressive religion is that it's less bad than the bigoted right-wing bullshit, but it still lends credibility to the idea that it's okay to believe things you have no good reason to think are true. They find out that we're atheists, not because we think religion is hostile and ugly, but because we think it isn't true. And the pro-atheist Kumbaya hand-holding dries up in a hurry.

I don't think the Kumbaya hand-holding is a facade. I think believers are sincere about it. It's just not closely examined. Many progressive believers have never talked with atheists about our atheism. So they make assumptions about what we think of them—and those assumptions are generally wrong. They assume we're as uncritically accepting of progressive religious groups as they are of each other. They assume our opposition to religion is simply to the bigoted, hateful, conservative versions—not to the whole idea of belief in the supernatural. They assume their particular beliefs get the Atheist Seal of Approval, that we admire their version of religion even if we don't agree with it. When they find out they're wrong, the "Thumbs-Up For Atheism!" attitude disappears into the mist. It was hard for me to see the smiles and applause and thumbs-ups at Pride, and not think about all those conversations and remember how they ended. It was hard to see the smiling approval and not think that ultimately, it was bullshit.

I didn't want to get into an argument. Actually—that's a stinking lie. I totally wanted to get into an argument. When the woman who was making nice said the religious right had gotten God's message all wrong, I wanted to ask her, "How do you know you're getting it right? You're both cherry-picking scripture—how do you know you're doing it right and you know what Jesus really meant? For that matter, what evidence do you have that Jesus is the son of God, or that he even existed?" I was dying to get into it.

And it would have been completely inappropriate. This wasn't a debate or a comment thread on my blog: this was Pride, and the whole reason I was there was to represent happy queer-positive atheism, not to get in a pissing match. So I smiled weakly, mouthed non-committal vagueness, and escaped from the conversation as gracefully as I could. Even this made me feel churlish. When people extend a hand and say we're all brothers and sisters, it feels rude to shrug and reply, "Yeah, not so much." When people are applauding you, it feels rude to not applaud back.

But I can't applaud religion. I just can't. I think religion is a flatly mistaken idea about the world, and I think it does significantly more harm than good. I can be friendly and respectful with believers, but I'm not going to cheer for their beliefs. And in a culture like the progressive LGBT world, where uncritical acceptance of different religions is standard etiquette, I don't know how to maintain that integrity without being read as pissy, intolerant, and churlish. Even if we're just being visible as atheists, we're still in their faces: there is no way to say we don't believe in God without implying that people who believe are wrong.

You know what, though? They're telling us we're wrong, too. When a believer comes up to an atheist and says, "God loves you," or even just, "I'm religious," they're telling us we're wrong to be atheists. If we're being churlish and divisive, so are they. If conversations are awkward, it's on them as much as it is on us. More, actually: they're the dominant culture, and they've set the terms of the conversation. The whole idea that religion is a special category, where criticism is off-limits and any differences are handled with kid gloves—that's their idea, not ours. And a lot of us are done with it. Atheist activists aren't just building communities and fighting bigotry. We're changing the terms of this conversation. We're putting religion on the table. Simply by being out and proud atheists, simply by keeping our integrity and refusing to be treated as second-class, we are changing the game.

If that's churlish, I can live with it.

CHAPTER THIRTY-SIX

Atheism and Friendship

How can we be honest about our atheism, and still remain close with people who are likely to be upset about it?

If you're figuring out how to be an atheist in a largely religious world, this is a really important question. But I'll be honest: I may not be the best person to ask. Most of my thoughts are about how I've screwed it up; how it's gotten screwed up anyway even when I don't think it was my fault; and how difficult it is to get right. My track record for discussing atheism with religious friends has been somewhat spotty, especially in my early days. But while I know I made mistakes, especially rookie mistakes early in my atheism career, I don't know that I did anything egregiously wrong.

This is a difficult subject. A lot of believers who think of themselves as open-minded and interested in atheists get more agitated about it than they'd expected. And they sometimes deal with that agitation by lashing out or pulling away. But regardless of whose fault it is, or even if it's anyone's fault, the bottom line is that almost every religious friend I've seriously discussed religion with has gotten mad at me. In a couple of cases, they're not even speaking to me. It's really sad. It's probably the hardest thing for me about being an atheist activist. And I honestly don't know whether I'm doing something wrong, or whether this is just going to be hard no matter what.

The way I'm currently dealing with it—a lesson learned from harsh experience—is to be honest about my atheism, but not to talk about it in great detail, or try to persuade anyone out of their beliefs, unless I'm explicitly asked to. At least, not if it's with someone I'm unwilling to lose. There's a difference between letting someone know what we think, and trying to persuade them to change their mind.

But even when we do draw that line, many believers will see any declaration of atheism as an attack. Even if we're just explaining why we believe what we do—even if we've been *asked* to explain that—many believers will take offense and think we're calling them fools. And when believers try to persuade *us* to change *our* minds, it's harder still to draw the line between defending atheism and persuading people that it's right.

As fucked-up as that is, it's also understandable. This line between explaining why we're atheists and explaining why God doesn't exist is a blurry one. No matter how carefully we talk about our atheism, we're still telling believers they're wrong. We need to accept that, and decide how to act on it.

I do draw a distinction between debating in public forums like Facebook, and doing it in personal conversation with friends. In public forums, I will happily explain my position at length, and do all I can to persuade people I'm right. But when it comes to talking about my atheism at parties or the dinner table, I don't usually do it that much unless I'm specifically asked to. And I tend to go easier, back off sooner, and change the subject more readily, than I would in public debate.

But not all believers draw this distinction. They often take public debates very personally, even when I consider them part of the marketplace of ideas. That's part of religion's armor. And even when I'm careful to critique ideas and not insult people, many believers have their faith deeply woven into their identity—so they take criticisms or questions about their beliefs as personal attacks. It's not fair, and in a public debate with strangers I won't give it any quarter. But with friends or family members we care about, sometimes we have to let things not be fair in order to keep the relationship. And sometimes we have to let go of relationships because we know they won't ever be fair. If there's anything I'd do differently now, I think it would be this. I'd recognize that religion is personal, that it can be hard to talk about—and I'd be more willing to drop a public argument with friends when it started to get upsetting.

There's another reason this is hard for me to write about: Atheism is a huge part of who I am. It's literally impossible for me to answer even casual small-talk questions, like "How's your work going?", without getting into the fact that I don't believe in God. This is my career, a big part of the purpose I'm creating for my life. I've made the hard, often sad choice that to pursue this path, I'm willing to lose some people I'd rather not lose. That's not true for everybody: lots of people who don't believe in God don't make a career out of it, and don't make it a core part of their personal and cultural identity. It's a little like the difference between coming out as gay and being a public gay activist. And the balance point that's right for me isn't necessarily right for you.

Sometimes, having a good relationship means striking a delicate balance between being honest about who you are, and not bringing things up that you know will be upsetting. It means deciding which parts of ourselves matter enough to us that we can't have a relationship if we can't be honest about them. It means deciding which topics should stay off the table and which are worth fighting for. That isn't just true about atheism: it's true about a lot of things. And it's not a simple all-or-nothing question. It's a question of nuance: how much to say, what exactly to say, who to say it to, how far to pursue it, when to drop it.

I don't always know how to do this. I'm getting better at it, but I get it wrong a lot, and even when I get it right, it's hard. If you have ideas, please let me know.

CHAPTER THIRTY-SEVEN

Compassion for the Religious

I posted the news on Facebook. A man had gotten stuck in a consensual but risky situation involving unconventional sexuality. He had called 911 for help—and his story spread all over the Internet when the 911 recording went public, with all the lurid details including his name. Atheists responded immediately: "We can't be soft on these people." "Their hijinks should be held up as an example." But this anger wasn't aimed at the people who'd leaked the recording, or the people gleefully dragging this man's private sex life through the Internet. The anger was aimed at the 911 caller, and these atheists were sharing the Internet's contempt and triumphant pleasure—because the 911 caller was a priest.

According to atheists on my Facebook page, this man had abdicated any right to call 911 without having his sex life splashed over the Internet. He was a hypocrite. He had supported an institution—the Catholic Church—that's created pointless sexual guilt for exactly the kinds of activities he was enjoying. And according to these atheists, his punishment should be the widespread public shaming of his private sexuality. They understood that there would be splash damage, that other people with unconventional sexualities would now be more afraid to call 911—and that was okay. That was acceptable collateral damage, a price they were willing to pay if we could expose a religious hypocrite. Another one. That week.

If you think I'm exaggerating, here are some other comments from that discussion: "I am glad he was humiliated." "These people bring it on themselves." "You deserve whatever embarrassment is heaped upon you when your hypocrisy is revealed." "It is his and his fellow clergy's fault that 'unconventional' sex is taboo. Fuck him." "Priests are terrorists and con-men." "When you know the history of these institutions, you have no sympathy for these people.... Fuck this wrinkled old sack of hypocritical horseshit."

I find this profoundly upsetting.

I am a passionate champion of atheist anger. I literally wrote the book on it.[1] Anger is a powerful tool in a social change movement. It motivates us to correct injustice, to alleviate harm, to make the world a better place. And I can absolutely understand the anger at the hypocrisy of church leaders who shame their followers for the exact sexual practices they partake in. I don't just understand that anger: I share it.

But there's a difference between anger and hatred.

When we're angry about religion, there's something we need to remember: The perpetrators of religion are also its victims. The people who traumatize young children with vivid and horrific images of hell were themselves traumatized by those horrors. The religious leaders who fill their flocks with ignorance and bigotry were themselves taught that these were divine virtues treasured by God. The people who warp the sexuality of their kids and teenagers, filling them with guilt and shame over perfectly healthy feelings, were themselves warped. The perpetrators of religion are also victims—and we're supposed to have compassion for the victims of religion.

When someone is a powerful, truly horrible perpetrator of religion—Osama bin Laden, Jerry Falwell, the Pope—the balance between compassion and anger will tilt heavily towards anger. It should. But a kinky priest giving himself pleasure condemned by his church? Is that an appropriate target for contemptuous, take-no-prisoners rage? Talk to the folks at the Clergy Project, the support organization for clergy who have become atheists. Ask them what it's like to be a member of the clergy who no longer believes their religion's teachings—whether that's "Kinky sex is bad," or "God exists." Talk to them about how trapped these people feel, how isolated, ashamed, afraid. Then tell me that they're terrorists and con artists, that you have no sympathy, that their hijinks should be held up as an example, that they deserve whatever embarrassment is heaped on them, and that you delight in their humiliation.

Our anger about religion is supposed to come from a place of compassion. It's supposed to come because we see so much harm coming from religion, and we desperately want it to end. When that anger turns into hatred, when it turns into sadistic victim-blaming, when it eradicates compassion for religion's victims because they're part of the toxic system, it has gone seriously wrong.

I do not want an atheist movement where anger at religion makes us lose all compassion for anyone involved in it. I do not want a movement where we reflexively hate all priests so much—without knowing anything about them—that we think it's okay for them to risk their life and safety rather than call for help. I do not want a movement where the public humiliation of religious sexual hypocrites is so important, we don't care that other people with unconventional sex lives are now even more afraid to dial 911.

Reading those Facebook responses was like seeing a caricature of atheism drawn by someone who hates atheists. But it was atheists drawing the caricature themselves. A self-portrait. And it's not a portrait I want any part of.

CHAPTER THIRTY-EIGHT

Is It Okay to Persuade Believers Out of Religion?

When atheists try to persuade people that religion is mistaken, are we being intolerant? When we work to change the world into one without religion, are we trying to create a drab, uniform world where everyone is just like us?

Many atheists are working to persuade believers out of their beliefs. I'm one of them. Many believers see this as an intolerant attempt to enforce conformity—particularly progressive interfaith believers who think all religions deserve respect. A fair number of atheists agree with them.

I don't agree. I vehemently don't. If you don't personally want to try to deconvert believers, that's fine with me—but those of us who do are not being intolerant. It's important to understand that, if we're going to engage with believers on equal ground.

The Intolerant Bigotry of the Germ Theory

If there's one idea I'd love to get across to believers, it isn't that there is no God, or even that there's probably no God. I want believers to reach that conclusion on their own. The idea I'd most like believers to understand is this: Religion is a conclusion about how the world works.

Religion is the conclusion that the world is the way it is, at least in part, because of supernatural beings or forces that act on the physical world.

Religion is many other things, of course. It's communities, cultural traditions, political ideologies, philosophies. But those aren't what make religion unique: you can have all that stuff without religion. What makes religion unique is belief in God, in gods, in spirits and demons and immaterial souls. What makes it unique is the conclusion that there is a supernatural world.

Religious belief is not a subjective opinion. It's a conclusion about objective reality. It says the world is the way it is because of God, because of Satan, because of the World-Soul, because spiritual energy is animating our consciousness, because guardian angels are watching us, because we are the reincarnated souls of the dead, because witches are casting spells. And since religion is a conclusion about the world, it's not intolerant to oppose it. Would it be intolerant to argue that germ theory is right and the four bodily humors theory is wrong? Would it be intolerant to oppose the idea that global warming is a hoax or that the sun orbits the earth? Arguing against conclusions that aren't supported by the evidence—that's not intolerant. That's how we understand the world.

Now, many believers will argue that religion doesn't fall into these categories. They'll argue that religion can't be proven true or false—so it's reasonable for people to believe in any religion that appeals to them. And it's unreasonable for anyone to argue against it.

That's not actually true. Many religious and supernatural beliefs, from young-earth creationism to astrology, do make testable claims. And every time those claims have been rigorously tested, they've folded like a house of cards in a hurricane. They can't be disproven with 100% certainty, but almost nothing can, and we don't use that standard of evidence for any other claim.

But some religions don't make testable claims, and can't be proven true or false. And once you start seeing religion as a hypothesis, the fact that it's unverifiable stops being a defense. A hypothesis has to be falsifiable. If any possible evidence could support it—the water in the beaker getting hotter, getting colder, staying the same temperature, boiling away instantly, turning into a parrot and flying out the window—your hypothesis is useless. It has no power to explain the past or predict the future. And that's just as true of religion. If any outcome of an illness could be explained as God's work—recovering dramatically, getting gradually better with medical intervention, getting worse, staying the same indefinitely, dying—the God hypothesis is useless. The fact that religion is unverifiable is one of the most devastating arguments against it.

And it isn't intolerant for atheists to point that out.

A New Model for Diversity

A lot of people still have problems with this form of atheist activism. Even if they know it's fair and reasonable, they still have an instinctive reaction against it. For a lot of people, it feels like religious intolerance to say, "Your religion is wrong, and I think you should change your mind about it."

I think the problem comes from how we think of religious diversity. Historically, we pretty much have two models of dealing with different religious views. We have intolerant evangelism and theocracy; forcing religious beliefs on other people through social pressure at best, legal strictures and even violence at worst. And we have uncritical ecumenicalism; the idea that all religions are at least a little true, that they're all part of a rich and beautiful spiritual tapestry, that they're all perceiving one piece of truth about God—and that even if they're not, it's bigotry to criticize them or try to persuade people out of them. Since that second model was created largely in response to the first, any criticism of religion gets seen through that harsh lens.

Atheism offers a third option.

Most atheists are passionate about the right to religious freedom. We fully support people's right to believe whatever the hell they want, as long as they keep it out of government and don't shove it in people's faces. The right to think what we like is a basic foundation of human ethics, and we have no desire to overturn it.

But our right to free thought and free expression includes the right to criticize. We can defend people's right to believe what they want—and defend with equal passion our right to think what *we* want about those beliefs, and to say what we think. There's no reason to treat religion with more deference than any other idea. Religion is a conclusion about the world, and there's no reason not to criticize it, ask hard questions about it, make fun of it, point out flaws in it, point out the good evidence contradicting it and the utter lack of good evidence supporting it, and do our damndest to persuade people out of it.

Some see this as evangelism. But the problem with religious evangelism isn't that they're trying to change people's minds. If you really think you're right about something important, of course you should try to share it. That's how good ideas get into the world. The problem with religious evangelism is that it tries to persuade using fear and false hope, and by shutting up any ideas that might contradict it. It tries to persuade by denying, ignoring, or even suppressing evidence; by using social pressure that makes people afraid to ask questions; by belittling the very idea that evidence should matter. And it refuses to accept that there are times when it's appropriate to change people's minds, and times when it's really not. It tries to win, not by playing fair, but by writing its own rules—and bullying people into accepting them.

The problem with religious evangelists isn't that they think they're right and are trying to change minds. That's the best thing about them.

Most atheists would probably be okay with a world that included religion, as long as it was tolerant of other beliefs and stayed the hell out of government. But many atheists would like humanity to eventually give up on religion. We think religion is a mistaken idea. We think we can make a good case for that position. We think it's reasonable to persuade people that we're right.

This is not an attack on diversity. It is a defense of reality.

CHAPTER THIRTY-NINE

Is It Okay to Mock Religion?

I got an interesting question a while back from Ola, a reader of my blog. She'd been talking with some believers about religion, and she'd made some points using parody religions like the Flying Spaghetti Monster and Kissing Hank's Ass. And the people she was talking with got upset. They said it was mean and disrespectful to mock their beliefs, and humor and sarcasm weren't arguments—they were cheap emotional tricks with no place in a meaningful debate. If you wanted to debate a serious topic, they thought, you should be deadly serious about it. Ola wanted to know what I thought: when we're discussing religion, is there a place for mockery?[1]

Let's start with the general principle: When discussing serious topics, is it ever okay to use humor? My answer is an unequivocal "Yes." From Aristophanes to Jon Stewart, from Mark Twain to Molly Ivins, from Chaucer to The Onion, satire is a powerful, time-honored form of social and political criticism. Humor and mockery can point out the pretensions and deceptions of the greedy, the pompous, the self-important, the hypocritical, the corrupt, the willfully ignorant—often more effectively than anything else. Humor shakes us up and gives us a different perspective, and when you're subverting the dominant paradigm or whatnot, that's crucial. When the emperor has no clothes, sometimes all you can do is point and laugh. And humor is fun, so people listen and keep coming back.

Mockery as legitimate social commentary? You bet! But is it okay to mock religion? I'm not asking if it's legally okay: of course it is, and in places where it isn't it should be. I'm asking if it's ethical, kind, or effective. And I don't think there's a simple yes or no. To get a nuanced answer, we have to ask some other questions.

What's the context? Public conversation is different from private conversation, and the social rules are different. Are we talking about mocking religion on your blog, or at Thanksgiving dinner? Are you mocking it in a letter to the editor, or is this a personal conversation with a friend? In public conversation, a harsher degree of criticism, both serious and sarcastic, is considered acceptable: if you don't believe me, look at political ads or movie reviews. The whole idea of the marketplace of ideas is that people speak, argue, joke, and change minds about ideas they like and don't like, and eventually the best ones catch on. (We hope.)

And when it comes to religion, public mockery isn't just acceptable. It can be a positive good. It can be a way of saying we won't treat religion with kid gloves anymore: that we see religion as just another idea, and when it's silly we're going to make fun of it. Treating religion with special respect armors it against valid criticism, and mockery helps strip it of that armor.

But in private conversation, ideas and information don't necessarily take precedence. Personal relationships and kindness to people you care about are often more important. If you're writing a fashion blog, you might say gaucho pants are a crime against humanity—but you probably wouldn't say it to your cousin Cindy who shows up at dinner wearing them. And I think that applies to religion. What's more, in public conversation it's easier for someone to turn away. If they don't like what you're saying, they can turn the page, change the channel, click to another blog. That's harder to do at Thanksgiving dinner. In situations where there's a strong expectation to not just get up and leave, it's both rude and unkind to make people choose between leaving, getting into a big fight, or sitting there and letting themselves be made fun of.

I'm not saying religion is off-limits in private conversation. I'm saying the tone should be different. Personally, unless I'm pretty sure everyone else in the room is a non-believer, I try to step lightly, speak tactfully, and choose my words carefully—more than I do in my public speech. I might still use humor, but I'll be more gentle with it.

Who or what is the target of the mockery? When I'm criticizing or mocking religion, there's a line I try to draw. I focus on beliefs and actions, not on people. I say things like, "Catholicism is ridiculous"—not "Catholics are fools."

Partly I do this because saying "Catholics are fools" veers dangerously close to bigotry. Because Catholics are so diverse, and vary so greatly in how much they adhere to the tenets of Catholicism, saying they're all fools is deriding people on the basis of the group they're in, instead of what they say and do. When we mock religious ideas and actions, we're participating in a noble tradition of satire as social criticism. When we mock religious people, we're part of an uglier tradition.

But I also draw this distinction because "Catholics are fools" is just not true. Catholics are no more or less intelligent than anyone else. They have some mistaken ideas about the world, but so does everyone. You don't have to be a fool to make mistakes, or even to hold on to mistakes in the face of overwhelming contradictory evidence. We all do that.

I make a few exceptions to this rule. When public figures make religion central to their public image, they're fair game for personal mockery—especially when they're hypocrites. But on the whole, I aim my mockery at ideas and actions, not people or groups.

What kind of mockery are we talking about? There's mockery that has a point. There's mockery that shines a brilliant, merciless spotlight on greed, hypocrisy, inconsistency, arrogance, willful ignorance, sloppy thinking, and flat-out evil. And there's mockery that just says, "Janie is a doo-doo-head." There's mockery that calls names and pokes fun without any content or point.

The latter is a lot less useful. It can have its place: it can be entertaining in the right context, and it can relieve tension and forge bonds within a movement. I'm certainly not going to say I've never indulged in it. But I don't have nearly the same respect for it that I do for the brilliant, merciless spotlight.

What are the power dynamics? Comedian Chris Rock made a famous distinction between punching up and punching down. In most of the world, religion is very privileged over atheism. But there's a world of difference between mocking a disenfranchised person who's relying on religion just to get through the day, and mocking the Pope.

Are you right? Is your mockery accurate and fair? I'm appalled at how many atheists will pass on a funny meme about religion—and when informed that it's incorrect, will defend it because it's funny and "sounds like something they would have said." The second you do that, you lose any moral high ground about reason, evidence-based thinking, and your passion for truth.

Finally:

What are you trying to accomplish? Are you trying to rally the troops? Are you trying to lift the spirits of atheists who already agree with you, and forge stronger bonds? Are you trying to inspire other atheists to get more involved, to take a further step into visibility and action? Are you trying to draw attention to atheism in the media and the public eye? Are you trying to shake religion off its pedestal, and get people to see it as just another view of the world that we can debate and mock?

Or are you trying to engage in fruitful debate? Are you trying to persuade believers to reconsider their beliefs—or at least their attitude towards atheists?

These are all valid goals. But they require different approaches. And in my experience, mockery is more useful for the first set of goals than the second. Very few people will be persuaded that they're wrong by being made fun of. Humor can work in a respectful, one-on-one debate, but in my experience, it has to be used more sparingly, and more lightly. It works better with less of a mocking, sarcastic, "don't you see what a fool you're being?" tone, and more of a gentle "we are all fools together" tone. There are atheists who say they were shaken out of their beliefs, in part, by hearing those beliefs mocked and seeing them brought down to earth. But generally speaking, making fun of people to their face tends to make them defensive, and entrenches them more stubbornly.

And if you don't agree, you're a doo-doo-head.

CHAPTER FORTY

Atheism and Patience

When atheists talk with believers, we often run into the same mistaken ideas, the same bad logic, the same forms of bigotry. We hear that atheists have no morality, no sense of meaning or purpose, no joy. We hear that atheists can't be 100% certain, so atheism is just as much a faith as religion; that science doesn't understand everything, so it's reasonable to think God exists. We hear that atheists are arrogant and that we aren't in foxholes. It gets a little old. As one of my commenters said, "Is it too much to ask for *new* bad arguments?"

But here's the thing I have to remind myself of, the thing I want to remind other atheists of:

These ideas are old to most of us. They're not necessarily old to believers.

Most believers haven't been hanging around atheist blogs for years. They haven't read a half dozen books about atheism, or indeed any. For many believers, these ideas are brand new. They've never carefully thought about atheists and atheism. They've never seriously questioned their beliefs, and we challenge those beliefs simply by being out as atheists. And they've never questioned the assumption that it's rude and intolerant to point out problems with religion, even in a public forum. As a result, many believers have never had to ponder hard questions about their beliefs—and their preconceptions of atheists have never run the reality check of actually talking with us.

So how often do we have to keep making the same points, and keep countering the same arguments? Pretty often.

Ingrid made a good point when we were talking about this. She said, "Imagine what it must be like to be a schoolteacher. You have to teach the same ideas, year after year after year. At some point you must just want to scream, 'Do I have to explain this again? Don't you know this already?' But of course, they don't. It's a new crop of students every year. It's old to you, but it's new to them."

And then there's the water on rock principle. I did a survey of atheists a while back, asking, "What finally convinced you? What finally made you decide that religion didn't make sense and atheism was more plausible?" And a huge number of people replied that it wasn't just one thing. It was a lot of ideas, a lot of arguments, adding up over time. That was certainly true for me. If I'd only heard these ideas once or twice, they would have been a lot easier to ignore or dismiss. Hearing them more than once forced them on my attention, and forced me to take them seriously.

So whether we're trying to persuade people out of religion, or are just trying to persuade people that atheists aren't miserable and evil, we have to keep making our points—and making them, and making them, and making them.

Patience doesn't mean continuing to beat your head against a brick wall indefinitely. There often comes a point when you have to be willing to drop it. If someone keeps repeating the same points over and over; if they don't respond to your ideas and are obviously ignoring them; if they keep bringing up red herrings; if they seem uninterested in logic and evidence; if they keep turning a discussion of actual issues into a meta-discussion about whether atheists even have a right to make our case; if they say things that are hurtful or hateful, and don't stop when you point out the hurt and hate; if they get upset; if *you* get upset—it's okay to bail. Part of being patient is knowing when to back off. Maybe you can pick up the conversation later. Maybe the seeds of doubt will have been planted, and someone else will pick up where you left off. Either way, there's no law saying we have to pursue every difficult conversation to the bitter end.

And patience doesn't mean being a doormat. We can and should make our case and speak our truth, and we should do it clearly. When we get accused of being intolerant, disrespectful, and mean just for doing that, it's totally reasonable to point out why that's absurd, unfair, and another way of shutting us up. And patience doesn't means we have to let ourselves be treated with genuinely insulting contempt.

What patience means is remembering that we're talking to human beings, and treating them that way. It means being careful to critique beliefs and ideas without insulting people. It means remembering that it's not fair to treat people like fools just because they're not familiar with the ideas we're intimately familiar with. It means keeping in mind how hard it can be to let go of religion. It means remembering that many of these folks are arguing because they're curious about us, or they care about us.

We all get to decide when to give up and when to keep going, and with whom. We get to decide when to take a break. We get to use our own judgment about who's genuinely unfamiliar with our ideas, and who's already heard them and is just being mulish. We get to decide which relationships will flourish with difficult but honest conversations, and which ones will do better if we leave some topics off the table. We get to decide who we want to maintain a relationship with at all. But the reality is that many people have bad, false, harmful ideas about atheism, and about religion. Many of these bad ideas are deeply ingrained; they're tightly woven into people's emotions and psychologies; entire social and political and economic structures are built on them. Changing people's minds is going to take time.

In twenty or thirty years, maybe we can start getting pissy with people who still make the "no atheists in foxholes" argument, the "you can't be certain" argument, or, for fuck's sake, Pascal's Wager. There'll come a point when nobody will be able to claim ignorance about this stuff. But as long as there are people who haven't heard our case, we have to keep on making it.

I know it gets tiresome. Boy, howdy, do I know. And no, it's not fair. Atheists are marginalized in much of the world, and being marginalized means dealing with ignorance, bigotry, and unfairness. But it's also not fair to treat all believers like fools.

CHAPTER FORTY-ONE

What Are the Goals of the Atheist Movement?

"It doesn't do atheists any good to criticize religion. In fact, it's counterproductive. It hurts our cause."

We see this argument a lot among atheists, and my typical response is to say, "Does not!" I point to history, and point out how other social change movements have successfully used both confrontation and diplomacy. I point to the Overton window—the idea of moving the center, with extremists making centrists look more reasonable—and I argue that confrontationalists make diplomats' job easier, not harder. I point out that firebrands are good at visibility, and visibility is crucial to countering myths and building community. I point out that while some people are more open to a calm, sympathetic voice, others tune into passionate cries for justice or a satirical jeer.

Here, I want to say something different. I want to ask: "Which goals are we talking about?" I don't think all atheists, even all atheist activists, have the same goals. And this may be the source of some of this conflict.

For many atheist activists, their primary goal is reducing anti-atheist bigotry and discrimination. Their main goal is to change people's minds about us: to get people to see us as happy, ethical, productive members of society, with equal rights and responsibilities. And they see firebrand atheists as feeding into the myths about us, alienating believers, and making their job harder.

But not all atheists see these as our main goals. For many atheists, the main goal is persuading the world out of religion.

Of course most atheist activists would love to see bigotry against us disappear. But many of us—I'm one of them—see that as only one of our goals. Many of us don't just want a world where believers and atheists get along. Many of us want a world without religion. We don't want this to happen by law or force, of course. But we think religion isn't just mistaken—we think it's harmful. Some of us think it's inherently harmful, that the very qualities that make religion unique are what make it capable of doing great damage. And we see religion not just hurting atheists, but billions of believers. We're working towards a world where it no longer exists.

If acceptance of atheists really were the primary goal for all of us, I might agree that we should dial back on criticizing religion. If our main goal is convincing the world that atheists are nice, getting in people's faces about how wrong they are might not be our best tactic. But that's not everyone's main goal. For many of us, getting legal rights for atheists and making sure they're enforced is more important. Many of us are more focused on building supportive atheist communities, which sometimes involves working with believers and sometimes doesn't. And for many of us, persuading people out of religion is our top priority. We think it helps achieve our other goals, and is valuable for its own sake.

If you disagree, about what our goals should be or how we should achieve them, let's have that conversation. But if you think criticizing religion is hurting our cause, you need to ask: Which cause? We may not be talking about the same one.

CHAPTER FORTY-TWO

The Power to Name Ourselves: Why I Don't Give a Damn If You Call Yourself Atheist, Agnostic, Humanist, Skeptic, Freethinker, Secular, or What

What should we call ourselves? When we say we don't believe in gods or supernatural beings, what word should we use?

Is "atheist" too negative, or too stigmatized? Is "agnostic" too wishy-washy? Is "skeptic" too widely misused? Is "humanist" too poorly understood? Is it too confusing to use "atheist" to mean anyone who doesn't believe in gods, even if they aren't 100% sure? Or to use "agnostic" for anyone who has just the tiniest fragment of doubt?

Of all the things our community can learn from LGBT history—and we have a lot to learn—this question is among the most important. Throughout history, other people got to name LGBT people. Being out was dangerous, and we couldn't use our own language in public. Apart from private talk with each other, we had to accept straight people's words. When they called us inverts, perverts, sodomites, the third sex—we had to shut up and take it. To this day, our earliest experiences include being hit with homophobic, biphobic, and transphobic slurs.

It's not just that other people named us. They got to define us. For decades, straight cisgender people defined what it meant to be homosexual, bisexual, transgender, and so on—and they insisted their definitions were right and ours were wrong, and that they knew us better than we knew ourselves.

And throughout history, other people got to decide which names for us were polite, and which were insulting. A classic example is the word homosexual. Most LGBT people don't like it: it's clinical, and it's connected with an ugly history of our sexuality being treated as a disease. But for decades, this was the "polite" word many straight people used, the word they thought of as neutral, regardless of how we felt about it.

Then when LGBT people started coming out in large numbers, and started openly pushing back against bigotry, part of that pushback involved saying, "We are not who you say we are. We are who *we* say we are." Naming has been a big part of that.

Because of all this, it's important to be able to name ourselves. It's important to choose our own names, and to decide what those names mean. "Bisexual," for instance, means somewhat different things to different bisexuals, and people who are attracted to more than one gender call ourselves a variety of names. When we're deciding whether we're bisexual, gay or lesbian, queer, straight, pansexual, or some other word, we focus on different things—our desires, our history, our wishes, our plans, who we're attracted to, who we fall in love with, if we've shifted throughout our lives, if we skew in one direction, and more. Deciding what to call ourselves can be deeply intertwined with deciding who we are—and what matters to us.

Because of all this, it's important to support each other's right to name ourselves. For instance: When gay men and lesbians insist that they know what "bisexual" means better than bisexuals, and tell people they're "really" bisexual or "really" gay or lesbian or straight, it perpetuates the exact same disempowerment we resist when we get it from straights.

It's true that naming ourselves can lead to confusion—especially in the earlier days of a community coming into its own, when a rough consensus about language is still forming. It can be confusing when not everyone uses this language the same way: it can be irritating when we say we're queer, or trans, or bisexual, or even gay or lesbian, and then have to spend ten minutes spelling out exactly what that means. But it's worth it. The power to name ourselves is too important.

So, similarly:

Non-believers shouldn't insist that we all call ourselves atheists, or humanists, or agnostics, or whatever. And we shouldn't insist that other non-believers define these words exactly the way we do.

I sometimes get puzzled by self-identified agnostics: most of them have the same uncertainty about God that they do about leprechauns. But if that fragment of doubt about God is important to them, or if there's less family conflict when they call themselves agnostic, I'm not going to insist that they're really atheists. And I want the same respect. I don't want agnostics insisting that my fragment of uncertainty means I'm really agnostic, or humanists insisting that my social justice work means I'm really a humanist. I'll decide that for myself.

The power to name ourselves is too important. We shouldn't try to take it from each other.

CHAPTER FORTY-THREE

What Does Religion Provide?

What do people get out of religion? Why do they like it? Why do they stay with it, even if they don't like it? And how can atheists provide the good things religion provides—so people who are questioning their faith will know atheism is a viable option, and people who do leave religion have a safe place to land?

This is something a lot of atheists and humanists have been asking ourselves: I think it's a hugely important question, and I'm delighted our community is responding to it. But I've started thinking that, vital as this question is, we should be reframing it. Asking what religion provides may not be that useful. Instead, we should ask ourselves, "What do people need?"

I'd like to reframe it this way for a couple of reasons. For one thing, I don't want to give religion any credit it doesn't deserve. I don't think religion actually provides all that much that people can't get in other ways. In fact, I would argue that there's exactly one thing religion uniquely provides—a belief in the supernatural. Everything else religion happens to provide—social support, safety nets, day care, rituals and rites of passage, a sense of tradition, a sense of purpose and meaning, counseling, networking, education and job training, activities for families, avenues for charitable and social justice work, events that are inspiring and fun, ongoing companionship and continuity—none of that is particular to religion. All of it can be gotten elsewhere.

But mostly, I'd like to reframe this question because I think it will help us be better organizers. I think it will help us be more nimble, and more flexible. What people need varies tremendously depending on their region, culture, subculture, upbringing, economic status, and their personality. And what people need from atheist communities varies just as much, depending on all those things and more.

In San Francisco where I live, there's *lots* of stuff available for people who aren't religious. There's social events, political organizing, charitable work, social justice work, activities and entertainment, all completely secular. So if people aren't religious, they don't have as much of a need for atheist community. And if people aren't religious here, they won't be treated as pariahs. There's sometimes conflict between atheists and believers—but coming out as an atheist here isn't a social death knell.

In the Bible Belt, that's a lot less true. A huge amount of socializing, charity work, social support, safety nets, economic and political networking, family activities, and so on are done through churches. You can't turn around without someone asking you, "What church do you go to?" Religion there is a hugely dominant force in people's day to day lives, and coming out as an atheist can mean becoming an outcast. It can mean losing your job, your home, custody of your kids, the love and support of family and friends. So atheists in San Francisco are, on the whole, going to have different needs than their counterparts in the Bible Belt.

When we started organizing the Godless Perverts in San Francisco, these questions were very much on our minds. The founders were talking about atheist communities in San Francisco and how we could draw more people. We thought out loud, "What will bring San Franciscans to an event? What do they like?" And the answer popped into our heads: "San Franciscans like sex." (Obviously other people like sex too, but folks here are generally more willing to be public about it.) So we started to put on events—a panel discussion, performance events, social meetups—exploring godless sexualities, and being generally blasphemous about sex and religion. We now have performance events three times a year, social meetups twice a month, and last December we held our first fundraiser party benefiting St. James Infirmary, the health clinic by and for sex workers.

Now, if we'd been asking what religion provides, we would never have come up with this. We would have come up with picnics, soup kitchens, coming-of-age ceremonies, something like that. There are lots of things religion traditionally provides, but explicit sexual entertainment is not generally among them. But because we were asking what people need and want—and were specifically asking what people in the Bay Area need and want—we could think outside the box, and come up with an idea Bay Area atheists responded to.

What people need from an atheist community in San Francisco is different from what they'll need in Tulsa. It'll be different in Austin and Manhattan, Minneapolis and Dallas, Montreal and Tokyo, Saskatoon and Seattle and Sydney and San Juan. If we keep asking ourselves what religion provides, we may focus too much on what religion already provides, and overlook creative ideas religion is generally missing. If instead we ask what people need, we'll be better able to meet those needs—the ones religion is currently filling, and the ones it doesn't have a clue about. And we won't be giving religion credit that it hasn't earned.

CHAPTER FORTY-FOUR

Why Do There Need to Be "Special Interest" Atheist Groups?

Why do there need be black atheist groups, women's atheist groups, ex-Muslim groups? Why should there be local groups, national organizations, online forums, for atheists with these identities or experiences?

This question comes up a lot, in almost every discussion I've seen of diversity in atheism. Many atheists are afraid these groups will splinter and divide our community. They see them as segregation or discrimination—exactly the things we're fighting against. And they don't understand why these folks can't just join a regular atheist group. A lot of people have given good, clear answers about their specific groups, and I recommend you read what they say.[1,2,3,4,5] But if you're wondering why there need to be special-interest atheist groups at all, ask yourself:

Why do you need an atheist group?

Why don't you just join "regular" groups? Why don't you join the Elks Club, the bowling league, the knitting circle, the book club, the Democratic Club, the Socialist Workers' Union, the PTA?

I know many of the answers. Because in those "regular" groups, you're likely to encounter anti-atheist hostility.

Because in those "regular" groups, even if people aren't overtly anti-atheist, they may unintentionally say or do things that are bigoted or ignorant.

Because in those "regular" groups, when you encounter bigotry or ignorance and try to educate people, they often refuse to listen, deny there's a problem, insist they've never seen a problem so it must not exist, and say you're being overly sensitive or are looking for a fight.

Because you don't always want to do Atheism 101.

Because even if nobody ever says anything bad about atheists, you still sometimes want to spend time with people who have experiences like yours.

Because your perspectives can be really different from those of believers: atheists often handle things like death, suffering, sexuality, social change, and other issues in ways that are very different, and it can be helpful to socialize with people who think more like you.

Because atheists' needs and interests are often different from those of believers, and groups that aren't atheist-specific often show a complete lack of concern.

Because even if nobody says anything bad about atheists, you still don't want to be the odd one out.

Because you want a place to strategize or vent about anti-atheist bigotry, or even to gripe about religion—and you don't feel comfortable doing that around believers.

Because an atheist group creates atheist visibility, and that does lots of good things. It lets other atheists know they're not alone, it helps us find each other, and it pushes back against stigma.

And because the whole idea that an atheist group somehow isn't a "regular" group is insulting.

I hope I don't have to spell this out, but I'm going to anyway: *Every single one of these answers also applies to "special-interest" atheist groups.*

Black atheists, atheist women, ex-Muslims, other specific atheist sub-groups, need our own groups because we want to spend time with people who share our experiences. Our groups create visibility and let others know we're here. We sometimes encounter bigotry and ignorance in "regular" atheist groups, and when we point it out we're ignored, gaslighted, and victim-blamed. We don't always want to do Race 101, Feminism 101, Islam 101. We sometimes have different needs and issues. Even if there were no prejudice or ignorance in a "regular" atheist group, being the only black person, the only woman, the only ex-Muslim, can still make us feel like the Other. You get the idea: I don't have to fill in every search-and-replace. The parallels aren't exact, of course: but a lot of the reasons are the same.

And it's important to point out: Plenty of "special interest" atheist groups are entirely uncontroversial. There are atheist parenting groups, book clubs, hiking clubs. There's an entire national organization, the Secular Student Alliance, devoted to the "special interest" group of atheist students. And in the years I've been involved in organized atheism, I have not heard a peep of complaint about these. I've never heard anyone ask, "Why do atheist parents need their own activities?" "Doesn't the atheist book club splinter and divide our community?" "Isn't the atheist hiking group segregation—discrimination against people who don't hike?" "Why do student atheists need a national organization? Why can't they just go to the regular off-campus atheist group?"

In fact, if these special interest groups can get enough members, it's seen as a good thing. It's a way to draw new people into our communities: if some atheists aren't interested in our other activities, but they like to hike or talk about books, these clubs might bring them in. And it's generally recognized that if a special interest group is flourishing, there's obviously a desire for it.

If you understand why atheists want atheist groups—and why atheist students, parents, and hikers want their own groups—you should understand why black atheists, women atheists, ex-Muslim atheists, want that as well. If you want them to feel welcome in your group too, support them in that.

CHAPTER FORTY-FIVE

Policing Our Own

(I am stealing this idea wholesale from Keith Lowell Jensen. Content note: harassment, threats of rape and other violence, domestic violence, child rape)

We want believers to police their own.

We want believers to stop being silent about atrocities committed in the name of religion. When religious families kick gay kids out of their homes; when theocrats force religion on others with law or violence or both; when husbands abuse their wives and justify it with God; when priests rape children and the church covers it up—we want believers to stop rationalizing, trivializing, and making excuses. We want them to stop treating in-group loyalty as the highest moral value they can imagine. We want them to speak out, to police their own. And when they don't, we call them hypocrites.

So why is it that when atheists speak out against screwed-up shit other atheists do, it gets called divisive?

I hear a lot of calls for unity in our community. When there are firestorms of debate about sexually invasive behavior at atheist events, about racist microaggressions in atheist communities, about misogynist and racist statements from atheist leaders who spout these attitudes for years, about transgender people being slurred and degraded by atheist public figures, about years-long orchestrated harassment campaigns against feminist women in the atheist movement, about sexual assault at atheist events—people ask why we can't all just get along. They say we agree ninety-five percent of the time, and despair that we keep arguing over the five percent we disagree about. They call on us to stop the infighting: they cry out about how it turns friends into enemies, drains our energy, weakens our movement. And I get it. I'm tired of the arguments, too.

But all too often, calling for unity means silencing dissent. It's a de facto defense of the status quo. It tells people who are speaking up for themselves to shut up.

I do not want to be in unity with atheists who tell me to fuck myself with a knife. I do not want to be in unity with atheists who tell me they hope I get raped, or to choke on a dick and die. I do not want to be in unity with atheists who say I'm a whore and nobody should take me seriously. I do not want to be in unity with atheists who say I'm an ugly dyke and nobody should take me seriously. I do not want to be in unity with atheists who post their opponents' home addresses on the Internet; who hack into their opponents' private email lists and make content from those emails public. I do not want to be in unity with atheists who bombard other people with a constant barrage of hatred and threats of rape, violence, and death. I do not want to be in unity with atheists who call me a cunt, who call other women in the movement cunts, again and again and again. And I do not want to be in unity with atheists who consistently rationalize this behavior, trivialize it, make excuses for it, or blame the victims.[1]

I don't think I should be expected to. I don't think anyone in this movement should be asking that of me—or of anyone.

I don't give a shit about the common ground I share with these people. The common ground of not believing in God is far less important to me than our differences. The five percent we disagree on is that they think it's okay to call women cunts, and I do not.

They think I should be ignored because I'm ugly or a whore, and I do not. They think it's okay to tolerate creepy sexual behavior and racist microaggressions in atheist communities, and I do not. They think it's okay to send up a Bat-Signal seen by millions and repeated for years, telling women and people of color that the atheist movement is a hostile environment and has no interest in giving them a home, and I do not. They think it's okay to hack into private email lists, and I do not. They think it's okay to gaslight victims of sexual assault, and I do not. They think it's okay to harass and threaten people, and I do not. They hope I get raped, and I do not. They want me to fuck myself with a knife, and I do not. These are the differences we're talking about. I reject the expectation that I should set them aside and focus on the common ground of not believing in God—and that I'm not being a good team player if I don't.

It is impossible for the atheist movement to be inclusive of everybody. We can't be inclusive of atheists of color, and of atheists who think people of color stay in religion because they're so emotional. We can't be inclusive of trans atheists, and of atheists who think trans people are mentally ill or freaks of nature. We can't be inclusive of atheists who are mentally ill, and of atheists who think mental illness is a failure of willpower. We can't be inclusive of atheist women, and of atheists who publicly call women ugly, fat, whores, sluts, cunts, and worse.

And when people, however well-meaning, make broad calls for unity—when they tell everyone to stop fighting and get along—they're telling the people on the short ends of those sticks to shut up. The cost of unity is the silence of people being screwed over.

We want believers to police their own. We need to stop trying to shut up atheists who are doing the same thing.

CHAPTER FORTY-SIX

More Rational Than Thou

It's great when atheists and skeptics criticize each other, and point out each other's mistakes in reasoning. That's supposed to be one of the cool things about us: we don't have sacred cows. We're willing, indeed eager, to question, be questioned, and change our minds if we're mistaken.

But there's a type of disagreement that's bugging me. It's when atheists and skeptics impugn each other's rationality about entirely subjective questions.

I've seen atheists argue that it's irrational to enjoy drinking; to follow sports; to care about fashion and style; to love our pets. They treat these preferences like questions of fact, open to scientific scrutiny, and they scold people for having the wrong ones. This is pointlessly divisive. I'm fine with being divisive if there's a point—I want us to debate our differences, I don't want us to march in lockstep—but pointless divisiveness, not so much. And these arguments are a misapplication of the principle of rationality. On subjective matters, an attitude of "more rational than thou" is, ironically, not very rational.

The day after Christopher Hitchens died, I posted an update saying, "Atheists around the world are getting soused tonight. This makes me oddly happy. Sort of a diffuse global community of drunkenness. I'll be joining them soon myself." And a commenter expressed irritation that the atheist community was embracing drunkenness, since it was anti-rational. When I asked what was irrational about pleasure, they replied that pleasure was fine—unless the way of reaching it kept you from thinking clearly.

There are some legitimate arguments to be had about drinking. "Drinking makes you irrational" isn't one of them.

There are plenty of things in life that make us behave irrationally. Falling in love. Singing. Riding a rollercoaster. Dancing all night. Playing with children. Playing with kittens. Jumping into an ice-cold pool. Eating an enormous, lavishly delicious meal. Having sex. Being gobsmacked by art. These are some of the finest, most meaningful experiences life has to offer. And it is not irrational to enjoy them. It is a reasonable conclusion, derived from an evidence-based analysis of what makes us happy.

A few years ago, Ingrid and I adopted kittens. From a strictly pragmatic standpoint, this was entirely irrational. Cats are expensive, time-consuming, they require significant re-arranging of our lives—and not at all trivially, *I am allergic to cats.* I have to be on meds around the clock. But we love having cats. They make us laugh uproariously. They make our hearts burst with love. They are one of our greatest pleasures. When we do the cost/benefit analysis of time, money, inconvenience, and allergies versus cuteness, entertainment, snuggling, and love, it falls squarely on the side of cats. It's not even close.

I could make a pragmatic case for pet ownership: there's evidence that it reduces stress and helps with depression. But even if that weren't true, I would still have cats. They make me happy. And when I'm talking about my own happiness, a subjective evaluation is the only one that matters.

In her excellent talk, "The Straw Vulcan: Hollywood's Illogical View of Logical Decision-Making," Julia Galef argues that the way pop culture depicts rational thinking is not rational at all: it's a caricature, a straw-man version of rationality. And she pointed out that atheists and skeptics often buy into these "straw Vulcan" myths: that the only rational goals are obviously pragmatic ones like money, and that a life of pure rationality is both achievable and desirable. But the reality, supported by extensive research, is that emotion is necessary for reason to work. We can work toward our goals with rigorous rationality—but without emotion, we have no way of deciding which goals to care about.[1]

Yes, I care about rationality. And if I have flaws in my reasoning about objective questions of fact, please tell me. I'll do the same for you. But if I get pleasure from drinking or sports, fashion or kittens, don't argue that I'm being irrational. If you do, *you're* being irrational. And in the great tradition of skeptical debate, I'm going to tell you about it.

CHAPTER FORTY-SEVEN

"There Is No Atheist Movement": Why I'm Done with Dictionary Atheism

"There is no atheist movement." "Atheism isn't a movement." "Look at the definition—all 'atheist' means is 'person who doesn't believe in any gods'! We don't have anything else in common! How can you build a movement around that?"

When I write about organized atheism, I get this response a fair amount. It's often called dictionary atheism, since it seeks to define atheism by the most narrow dictionary definition. I see the idea a lot—and I'm so far beyond done with it, I could scream.

Let's talk about the gay rights movement. (In this particular context, I don't mean LGBT.) Technically, the only thing gay men and lesbians and bisexuals all have in common is that we're attracted to people of the same gender—but we've built a movement. We've built organizations that push back against the discrimination and bigotry we all share. We've built organizations to amplify our voices, knowing these are all too easily drowned out. We've built organizations to preserve our history, knowing this is all too easily destroyed and lost. We've built organizations to educate straight people, and to counter the myths, fears, and misinformation about us. We've built networks to educate each other about job discrimination laws, anti-gay violence, coming-out techniques, safer sex, and hundreds of other issues that affect us.

We've built support structures and supportive communities to replace those we'd lost. I could go on.

Technically, the only thing gay men and lesbians and bisexuals all have in common is that we're attracted to people of the same gender. And if we'd decided we couldn't build a movement around that, we'd be in the crapper. Forget same-sex marriage and employment non-discrimination: we'd still be getting put in mental hospitals, getting our bars shut down by police, getting arrested for looking too gay. We haven't just built a movement. We've built a powerful movement that radically improved our lives and has had a significant impact on society at large.

Is there any reason LGB people can organize, but atheists can't? Is there some reason same-gender attraction can be an effective locus for community and political organizing—but disbelief in gods can't be?

Of course there's an atheist movement. There's the Foundation Beyond Belief. The Secular Student Alliance. The American Humanist Association. The Freedom From Religion Foundation. American Atheists. Atheist Alliance International. Black Non-Believers. Hispanic American Freethinkers. Secular Woman. The United Coalition of Reason. Council of Ex-Muslims of Britain. Ex-Muslims of North America. Grief Beyond Belief. Recovering From Religion. Filipino Freethinkers. Sunday Assembly. Atheist Foundation of Australia. Kasese United Humanist Association. Pakistani Atheists and Agnostics. The Secular Therapist Project. The Clergy Project. Godless Perverts. The Center for Inquiry. The many local chapters of Center for Inquiry. 1,120 (as of this writing) atheist groups on Meetup. Many many many many more. And none of that includes atheist organizing and community-building online: Atheist Nexus, ExChristian.net, Skepchick, the Patheos Atheist channel, Freethought Blogs, The Orbit, much more.

What the heck is all that if not an atheist movement?

If you want to argue that there shouldn't be an atheist movement—knock yourself out. But don't argue that there isn't an atheist movement. There is. There is a movement dedicated to promoting the rights of atheists, countering the myths and bigotry against atheists, sharing and spreading ideas about atheism, creating supportive communities for atheists who have left religion, and more. That's the reality. And atheists should not be in the business of denying reality.

As Bad Willow said on *Buffy the Vampire Slayer*: Bored now. I am done arguing whether an atheist movement exists. I'm just going to get on with helping make it happen.

THE GOOD LIFE: SEX, LOVE, PLEASURE, AND JOY

CHAPTER FORTY-EIGHT

Atheist Thoughts on a Life Well-Lived

With no gods and no afterlife, what makes for a life well-lived?

For many believers, a good life is framed in external terms, and as forward motion. It means making their god happy, and getting to some happy afterlife. In fact, believers are often baffled about how atheists can experience meaning when we don't have God deciding it for us, and when we're not charging through this life to reach the next one.

But even in a secular context, we often think of a meaningful life as a life with direction. We think of it as raising children; creating art; building and growing a business; making the world a better place. These are all good ways to live: I'm deeply engaged in more than one of them. I'm a driven, forward-moving person, and I do tend to think of the meaning of my life in terms of where it's going, what I'm achieving, and what I'll leave behind when I die.

But these aren't the only good ways to live. A life well-lived doesn't have to be a life with accomplishments. It can be a life with experiences. We can see the value of our lives, not just in where we're going, but in where we are, and where we've been.

A life well-lived can simply be an interesting life; a life with adventures, hobbies, books, music, travel, sex, friendships, love. It can have an upward-and-forward career trajectory, or a series of weird-ass jobs. It can be spent building and improving a home, or living in a dozen different cities. It can be devoted to making the world better for more people, or getting to know some of those people. It can focus on solid accomplishments, or interesting hobbies. It can have shelves full of books you've written, or full of books you've read.

And frankly, if there aren't people to experience stuff, what point is there to the accomplishments of all the accomplishers? As a writer, my life's work is only meaningful if there are readers. A musician's work is given value by music lovers. An architect's work has purpose because of people living and working in their buildings. Accomplishment and creativity are two-way streets: they require a recipient to make the connection. And it's the connection that makes them meaningful.

If atheists are going to say that we create our own meaning, and that life is meaningful and precious without a creator or an afterlife, we should let go of the teleological thinking that's inherent to religion. A good life can mean many things, and move in many directions. It doesn't have to constantly move forward.

CHAPTER FORTY-NINE

Atheism and Sensuality

Let's talk about a pleasant topic for once. The most pleasant topic of all, in fact. Let's talk about pleasure.

The atheist view of sensuality, of pure physical pleasure and joy in our bodies, is a thousand times better than any traditional religious view. Our views of physical pleasure are more coherent, more ethical, and way the hell more appealing and fun. We don't believe in a supernatural soul that's finer and more important than our bodies. We don't think we have a soul separate from our bodies, period. We sure as heck don't believe in an immaterial god who thinks our bodies are icky—even though he, you know, created them—and who makes up endless, arbitrary, unfathomably nitpicky rules about how we may and may not use them, what food we can eat, what clothes we can wear, what sex we can have. We understand that the physical world is all there is. We understand that our bodies, and the lives we live in them, are all we have. As a result, we are entirely free—within the constraints of basic ethics, obviously—to enjoy these bodies, and these mortal, physical lives. As atheists, we're free to celebrate our bodily pleasures as thoroughly and exuberantly as we can.

So why don't we?

Why isn't atheist culture more physical? Why isn't it more focused on sensuality and sensual joy? Why is it so cerebral so much of the time? As atheists, we've rejected the idea that there's a higher, finer world than the physical one. Why does it so often seem as if we've bought into it? Dr. Anthony Pinn posed this question at the 2012 Atheist Alliance of America conference, and it's been tumbling in my brain ever since.

I know for a fact that many individual atheists, maybe even most of us, don't live this cerebral way in our private lives. I know I'm not the only atheist who revels in good food and better hooch; who fucks all afternoon and dances all night; who walks in the sun for miles and pumps iron for the sheer endorphiny pleasure of it; who literally stops and smells roses. But our public life typically doesn't reflect this. There are exceptions, of course: karaoke parties at conferences, Skeptiprom, Godless Perverts. But in large part, our public life as atheists—our community events, online forums, writings, billboard campaigns, outreach campaigns, our culture—is geared toward political activism, social change, science, and the life of the mind.

Don't get me wrong. I am a passionate devotee of all these things. But that's not all atheist culture has to offer. Not by a long shot. This notion that our selves are not separate from our bodies, and therefore this life is all we have, is one of our greatest strengths. And yet, in public at least, we flinch from one of its most obvious logical conclusions—the idea that ethically pursued pleasure not only isn't sinful, but is a positive good. When believers accuse us of being sybaritic hedonists, we hotly deny it, rather than saying, "Hell yes, we're hedonists, why shouldn't we be?" When believers insist we've rejected God's rules just so we can wallow in sensual pleasure, we get all high-minded and offended, and cite every other reason we can think of for rejecting religion, rather than saying, "Yup, that's part of it. Your made-up god's rules about pleasure are inconsistent and ridiculous, they do real damage, and for a lot of us they're part of why we started questioning religion." When believers accuse us of the dreaded crime of enjoying our bodies, we defend ourselves against the accusation rather than question the premise behind it.

What's that about?

Some of it may just be PR. In the United States, the Puritanical equation of pleasure with sin is deeply ingrained. Some atheists think that to gain acceptance in mainstream culture, we have to accept that culture's values, or at least not make a virtue of flouting them in public. But this isn't just about public image—it's about how we see ourselves.

It's common for marginalized people to buy into worldviews that marginalize them. Internalized sexism, racism, homophobia, and so on are well-documented, and that shouldn't be a surprise. We're all soaking in these attitudes—even the people targeted by them—and we all absorb them. And this is just as true for atheists. Our own discomfort with atheism can be overt, as we see with atheists who think faith is wonderful and necessary and they wish they had it themselves. And sometimes it can be subtle, an unconscious absorption of less obvious ideas—like the acceptance of the preposterous notion that physical experience is less valuable than intellectual experience, and that physical pleasure is shameful.

Let's knock it off. Let's celebrate our bodies as much as we do our minds. In fact, let's stop seeing our bodies as something apart from our minds. Let's not simply reject Cartesian dualism, and the absurd notion that the soul is the real self and the body is just a skanky shell. Let's reject its mutant offspring—the absurd notion that the intellect is the real self and the senses are just a meaningless indulgence.

The atheist view of physical pleasure is more coherent, more ethical, and way the hell more appealing and fun. And it has the advantage of being the truth. Let's put that view front and center.

CHAPTER FIFTY

To Give Itself Pleasure: An Atheist View of Sexual Transcendence

How can we experience sexual transcendence without belief in the supernatural?

If you're investigating secular sexuality, you may have already found the sex-positive community—and found that it's often very spiritual. It's not conventionally religious (usually), but many varieties of New Age belief, spiritual-but-not-religious belief, and magical thinking are widespread. These beliefs get blended into both private sex lives and public work, such as writing, workshops, and activism. And the fusion of spirituality with sexual transcendence often gets framed, not just as feasible, but as necessary, with those of us who don't believe left pressing our noses against the glass to gaze at the party inside.

I want to offer an alternative.

The materialist view says there is no supernatural world. At all. There is only the physical world. All those things that seem non-physical—thoughts, feelings, choices, selfhood, transcendent sexual ecstasy—are products of the brain, and of the brain's interactions with the rest of the body and the world. We don't yet know exactly how this works, the science of neuropsychology is still in its infancy, but the evidence is overwhelming. Whatever consciousness is, it's physical.

To me, that is not a downer. That is magnificent. Out of nothing but earth and water and sunlight, wildly complex living beings developed, not only with consciousness but with the capacity to create ecstasy for ourselves and one another. Magnificent.

Carl Sagan once said, "We are a way for the cosmos to know itself." That is both true and mega-cool. 13.7 billion years ago the universe went Foom—it's gone through countless configurations since, and one of those is conscious life, curious life, life that's looking around, comparing notes, and figuring out what's going on.

But we aren't just a way for the universe to know itself. We are a way for the universe to give itself pleasure. When we have orgasms, we are shifting the matter and energy of the universe into the form of euphoric, all-encompassing bliss. When we fuck, suck, lick and finger and spank, masturbate, tie each other up, when we make good porn and enjoy good porn, when we dress up like saloon girls or ponies or 1950s bikers, we are the universe getting itself off.

And we don't just experience our own pleasure. We experience each other's. We can give each other orgasms, and take pleasure in them. We can finger each other's pussies and suck each other's dicks and spank each others asses, and have it flood our brains with the chemicals of joy. As hungry as we are for our own pleasure, we can also be desperately, feverishly hungry for each other's. We are a miniscule piece of the matter and energy of the universe, looking carefully at some of the rest of the matter and energy, and asking, "How would you like to get off?"

Sex connects us with ourselves, with each other, with the universe—and it connects us with life. Transcendent sexual joy is hard-wired into our brains by hundreds of millions of years of evolution—or, to put it more crassly, orgasms feel good because animals are more likely to reproduce if they really want to boff. So sex connects us with every living thing on earth. We are the cousins of all living things on this planet, with a common ancestor of primordial soup going billions of years back—and we are all related, not entirely but substantially, because of sex. That is awesome. That makes me want to go fuck right now, just so I can feel connected with my fish and tetrapod and primate ancestors. That is entirely made of win.

And I love that we've taken this powerful evolutionary drive, and have taken ownership of it. Many of the most beautiful, valuable parts of human experience happen when we take deep evolutionary wiring and transform it into something beyond prosaic survival and reproduction. We took our need for palatable food, and turned it into chocolate soufflés; we took our ability to make and use tools, and turned it into the Apollo moon landing; we took our uniquely precise ability to communicate through language, and turned it into *King Lear*. And we've done the same for sex.

I love that we've taken this drive, and have said, "Sure, this was once about reproduction, and sometimes it still is—but it doesn't have to be. This can be about anything we want, with anyone who wants it." I love that we've dressed it up in studs and feathers, boots and stockings; that we've added private roleplay and public theater; that we've spent millennia exploring it in painting and writing and film and pixels. I love that we can use this drive to turn pain into ecstasy, shame into intimacy, helplessness into adventure, power into trust. I love that we've blended this drive with our ability to make and use tools, in the form of dildos and vibrators and buttplugs and floggers and condoms and lube and violet wands and things I can't even identify. I love that we've blended this drive with our ability to learn, explore, and understand, in the form of books and videos and workshops and research papers and blogs, about anatomy and sociology and psychology and sexology, about birth control and the psychological health of queer people and how exactly you tie someone to the bed. I love that we've blended this drive with our unique capacity for language, so we can say to each other, "What I like is feathers and boots and floggings and vibrators and getting tied to the bed. What do you like?" I love that we've taken this powerful evolutionary drive, and transformed it into expressions of love, friendship, companionship, consolation, community, intimacy, art. In the words of Darwin, although not about this subject exactly—endless forms most beautiful.

And finally:

When you don't believe in God or the soul or any sort of afterlife—when you believe this short life is all we have—then making the most of that short life, and taking advantage of its joyful experiences, suddenly becomes a lot more important. The odds against you, personally, having been born into this life, are beyond astronomical. Are you going to waste that life by not giving yourself, and other people, as much joy as you can?

We don't need to see sex as blessed by the Goddess, a connection between souls, a channeling of chi energy, or any form of worship or spiritual practice, to see it as valuable. We can see sex as a physical act between animals, and still see it as richly valuable and meaningful. We can see sex as a physical act that connects us intimately, not only with ourselves and one another, but with all of life, with the expanse of history, and with the vastness of the universe.

CHAPTER FIFTY-ONE

My Vision for a Sexual World

Music. I want us to treat sex like music.

I want to present a vision for the sexual culture I'd like to see. Like a lot of sex-positive writers, I spend a lot of time ranting about things in our sexual culture I don't like: that's worth doing, but I don't want to tear down if I don't have something to build. So here's my castle in the air—based on the world we live in, a world we know is possible. I want us to treat sexuality, and differences between sexualities, much the same way we treat music.

We have a basic acceptance of the idea that different people like different music. We may strongly dislike the music other people like. We may even make unfair judgments about people who like opera, country, rap, Barry Manilow. But as long as people aren't forcing their music on us, we usually accept—if grudgingly—their basic right to listen to any music they like.

I'd like to see us do the same with sex. If people are personally grossed out by gay sex, or sadomasochism, or furries, I certainly would recognize their right to be. I just want people to see their gross-outs as personal tastes—not moral judgments.

We understand that some people don't care about music, and some people care about it a great deal. We understand that some people care about music so much they make it central to their lives. People collect music, read about it, write about it, play it, watch performances of it, find inspiration and consolation in it, build friendships and relationships centered on it. Some people even make a living at it. And we understand that for some people, music is just not that big a deal. Some people don't respond to it or care about it at all; others like it fine, but don't make a big place for it in their lives.

I'd like to see us have the same understanding about sex. I'd like to see us treat people who like sex a lot and are very interested in it as… well, people who like sex a lot and are very interested in it. Not as moral degenerates, not as selfish indulgers of our own petty whims, not as dangerous or pathetic addicts unable to control our base impulses, but as people whose interest in this common human activity happens to be greater than average. And for all of us sex fiends, I'd like to see us have a similar understanding about people who aren't interested in sex at all, or aren't as interested as we are.

We understand that people's tastes in music often change over time. We don't expect people in middle age to like the same music they did when they were in high school or college; and while many people do stay mostly interested in the music of their youth, we understand that many other people continue to explore different kinds of music throughout their lives, and may even find their preferences changing entirely over time. And we understand that some people like a wide variety of musical styles, while other people's tastes tend to stay within one genre.

I'd like us to have the same understanding about sex. I'd like to see us recognize and accept that not everyone stays slotted in the same sexual category for their whole life: people's desires, even our basic orientations, can change over time. When gay or lesbian people decide they're bisexual or pansexual; when bi or pan people decide they're more straight or gay; when vanilla folks decide to try spanking; when committed polyamorists decide they want to be monogamous for a while, I'd like us to recognize it as the kind of natural change people go through in life. If it affects us personally—if it's our lover or spouse who suddenly announces they're into men or spanking or monogamy—of course our reactions will be different. But if it's not about us, I'd like us to see it as... well, not about us. We might see it as interesting, but we'd also understand that it's none of our business.

In relationships, we often see music as one of the main bonds between us. When we get involved with someone new, we get excited about sharing music; getting them to listen to our favorite band, discovering music they love that we've never heard. We sometimes have conflicts with our honeys over differences in musical taste, especially early in a relationship; but we talk about it, joke about it, find ways to enjoy our differences as well as our common ground. And as our relationships grow, we often explore new music together.

I'd like us to see sex the same way. I'd like for sex to be something we can talk about comfortably in relationships, and laugh about. I'd like for people to explore sexual differences as well as similarities; not just early on in relationships, but as things grow and change. I'd like people in relationships to see sex as something that's worth working on. And if there are differences in what kinds of sex people like, or how much they even care about sex, I'd like for everyone's tastes and desires to be treated as equally valid and important—by each other, and by their friends, support systems, and society.

And finally:

We understand—or at least, we're beginning to—that music is a basic human activity, and for many people a basic need. We understand that music exists in all human societies, and has for tens of thousands of years. We understand—or we're beginning to—that music is fundamental to how most of our brains and our minds operate.[1] We see music as an activity that is both necessary and joyful, a vital social bond, something that connects us to our history and projects us into our future.

I'd like us to see sex the same way. I'd like us to see sex as something we couldn't possibly get rid of, and wouldn't want to get rid of if we could. I'd like us to recognize that sex is one of the most fundamental parts of how most human minds are wired, one of the chief lenses we see the world through. I'd like us not only to recognize this fact, but accept and even celebrate it. I'd like us to remember that sexual reproduction is a link that connects us to the chain of human history and the web of life. It's how most of us got into this world, and for many of us, it's one of the chief ways part of us of will live on after we die. I'd like us to see sex as one of the great joys, inspirations, consolations, forms of communication, forms of connection, and just pure forms of entertainment the human race has.

And I'd like us to give it some respect.

I understand this analogy isn't perfect. Sex and music work differently in our brains, and they play different roles in our evolution. Sex goes back hundreds of millions of years, and almost every animal species has some form of it: it's probably always going to be highly charged and emotionally loaded. And sex has more potential than music to cause harm; from sexually transmitted infections to unwanted pregnancies, jealous rages to broken hearts. With some exceptions—irritated neighbors, advertising jingles, sexist song lyrics, neo-Nazi death metal—music just doesn't have the same power to hurt people.

It's not a perfect analogy. But it's a start. We're going to build a better sexual future. Let's start by looking at a part of life we mostly get right.

CHAPTER FIFTY-TWO

"Nothing to Do with Destined Perfection": An Atheist View of Love

What does it mean to have a skeptical view of love?

I don't mean a cynical view. I mean a materialist, non-supernatural one. I've been thinking about the idea of romantic destiny, and of there being one perfect soulmate for you in the whole world. I think it's crap. And I don't think I'm being unromantic. Quite the opposite.

The whole soulmate/romantic destiny thing is just wrong. We don't have souls, much less mates for them. There's no invisible hand pushing people together, and if there were, it'd have a seriously sadistic sense of humor, what with putting people's true loves on opposite sides of the world.

But more to the point: The notion of romantic destiny sees love as something we feel, rather than something we do; something that happens to us, rather than something we choose. And I find it much more romantic, and much more loving, to see love as something we do, and something we choose.

When we see love solely as something we feel, what happens when those feelings change? They always do. And when we see love solely as something that happens to us, what happens when the going gets tough and we have to make hard choices? What happens when we get job offers in other cities—or, if we're monogamous, when other romantic prospects come on the scene?

Of course a huge part of love is how we feel about our beloveds. The feelings of tenderness and passion that well up in me when I look at Ingrid, the anxious excitement I felt when we were starting out—that's an enormous part of what we have. And of course, a huge part of love can be the feeling that something's hit you out of the blue. When Ingrid and I were first going out, it felt like I'd been conked on the head with a giant vaudeville rubber mallet. If love didn't have the power to knock us out of our tracks and into a whole new life, it wouldn't be what it is.

But that's not enough. It gets love started—but it's not enough to sustain it.

What sustains love is doing the dishes when you promised to. Remembering the book they wanted, and getting it for their birthday. Skipping the movie you wanted to see, to go with them to a party of their friends who you don't know very well. Remembering which kind of seltzer water they like when you go shopping; remembering how they like their burgers cooked when you're making dinner. Sitting with them when they're grieving—and restraining your impulse to always try to fix things and give advice and make things better, and instead just sitting still and being with them in their pain. Asking if there's anything they need from the kitchen while you're up. Wearing the annoying sticky breathing strip at night so your snoring doesn't keep them awake. Bringing endless cups of tea when they're sick. Keeping your temper in an argument, and remembering that as angry as you might be right now, you love this person and don't want to hurt them. Saying, "I love you." Saying, "You're beautiful"—not just when they're dolled up for a night on the town, but when they come home from work and you notice that they look particularly fetching. Noticing when they look particularly fetching. Going to their readings, their dance performances, their office parties. Going to their family gatherings, and treating their family as yours. Going to the vet together. Trying out music they like, books they like, recipes they like, hobbies they like, kinds of sex they like, even if you don't think it's your thing—not just to make them happy, but because it's part of who they are, and you want to find out more about them and share the things that matter to them.

Love is sustained by the things we do, and the things we choose.

In the inimitable words of atheist musician Tim Minchin, "Love is nothing to do with destined perfection/ The connection is strengthened; the affection simply grows over time."[1] What I feel for Ingrid has a lot to do with the giant vaudeville mallet I got conked with when we fell in love. It has more to do with the eighteen years we've spent together—the meals we've eaten, parties we've thrown, vacations we've taken, arguments we've had, sex we've had, griefs we've borne, thousands of nights spent in the same bed, thousands of long conversations about politics, religion, books, our friends, our cats, bad reality TV.

And none of that has anything to do with fate.

I am intensely aware of the massive role that chance plays in our lives. Not fate, not destiny, but random, roll-of-the-dice luck. As passionately as I love San Francisco, I could have landed in a dozen other cities—New York, Portland, London, Amsterdam, Minneapolis—and happily settled there instead. I often think about the people in those cities who would be my friends if I lived there; sometimes I even feel a loss, a yearning, for all the best friends I never met.

And I realize that if I'd wound up in one of those cities, I never would have met Ingrid, and we'd probably both have fallen in love with other people instead. While there's a pragmatic sense in which I suppose we were destined to meet—we live in the same city, we're interested in many of the same things, we know a lot of the same people—any one of a thousand small choices and bits of random chance could have resulted in our paths not crossing, or not crossing at the right time. Different choices, different slivers of chance, and we could have ended up with other people—people we probably would have been happy with, people who might have been less well suited for us in some ways but better suited in others, people who, as Tim Minchin sang, fall within a bell curve.

The idea that, out of the billions of people in the world, there is one and only one I could have loved and been happy with? It makes no sense. And it trivializes the work and the love we've put into creating what we have.

What makes Ingrid unique to me isn't that she's my soulmate, my destiny, the one person in billions I could have loved and been happy with. What makes Ingrid unique is the years we have behind us, the meals and parties and sex and conversations and trips to the vet and everything else. It's the things we do and have done, and will do for many more years to come. It's the choices we make, and have made, and will make in the years we have left.

Of the people in the world I might have been happy with? She falls within a bell curve. Of the people in the world I now want to be with? She is unique. Not because a divine hand made us perfect for each other—but because we have chosen to make each other unique.

CHAPTER FIFTY-THREE

Intransitive Gratitude: Feeling Thankful in a Godless World

A few years ago, the Fellowship of Freethought Dallas put together a video, asking participants at Skepticon 4 to say what they were thankful for. Most of the folks in the video, myself included, took the question at face value, and spoke of our intense gratitude for science and medicine, friends and family, jobs in an unstable economy, trees, the fact that we exist at all.[1]

But one participant, PZ Myers, questioned the entire assumption behind the project. PZ said that asking people to be thankful for something was an attempt to "anthropomorphize the universe." He said there were lots of things he liked—being alive, his wife, his kids, squid—but he wasn't going to express gratitude to the universe, since the universe wasn't capable of expressing gratitude back.

Interesting point.

So this video got me thinking: If you don't believe in God, does it even make sense to say you're grateful for stuff? I don't mean being grateful to specific people for specific things: that kind of gratitude obviously makes sense. I mean general gratitude for good things in our lives. Does gratitude need to have a particular object, a conscious actor who made choices that affected our lives in positive ways? Or can we feel grateful without thanking anyone?

Is there such a thing as intransitive gratitude?

My friend Rebecca Hensler (founder of Grief Beyond Belief) once said that for her, one of the hardest things about becoming an atheist was figuring out what to do with feelings of gratitude. She used to express these feelings through spiritual practices, but when she let go of her spiritual beliefs, those feelings were left without an object. And that left her feeling oddly uncomfortable.

Until she said this, I hadn't thought of it in those terms. But I immediately knew what she meant. I have a strong awareness of having good things that I haven't earned, or that I have earned but are also the result of luck. In fact, most good things in my life are partly the result of luck. Sure, I have some good things because I'm smart—but I was lucky to be born into a family that prioritized education and valued intelligence. Sure, I have good things because I work hard and have a certain amount of self-discipline—but I was lucky to be born into a privileged race and economic class, where I've had opportunities for my hard work and discipline to pay off, and where I've had enough slack that I could occasionally make mistakes without it screwing up the rest of my life. Sure, I have good things because I'm a reasonably good person—but I was lucky to be born into a life that didn't bludgeon the kindness and empathy and generosity out of me at an early age.

I have a strong awareness of having good things I didn't earn. Including, most importantly, my existence. And it feels wrong not to express this awareness. It feels churlish, entitled, self-absorbed. I don't like treating my good fortune as if it's my due. I think gratitude is a good thing. Gratitude is intimately connected with our sense of fairness and justice. It's how we know the scales have tipped in our direction, and it's what inspires us to balance that scale and give others their due. That's a good thing. I would never try to talk people out of it.

But PZ has a point. If there's no target for our gratitude, we're prone to making one up. We anthropomorphize the universe, and see purpose behind random chance. And that can contribute to the massive, destructive error that is religion.

Our sense that the world should be fair, that we should repay the good things that come our way and be compensated for the bad ones, makes sense in the world of human interaction. But when it's taken outside that context, when that feeling doesn't have an object, it can get twisted. It can lead us to make pointless sacrifices to non-existent gods, killing animals or cutting off our children's foreskins as a way to say "Thanks" to our imaginary friends in the sky. It can lead us to think the vagaries of our lives are divine punishment or reward—torturing ourselves trying to figure out why we're being punished, or feeling smugly entitled to our good fortune and assuming that if we have it, we must have earned it. It can lead us to think that the vagaries of other people's lives are divine punishment or reward; accepting gross inequalities as God's will, or making us callous and judgmental about the suffering of others.

So intransitive gratitude might not be such a good idea. Maybe "grateful" isn't even the right word here.

Maybe a better word would be "fortunate."

That's a useful distinction. When people consciously act to make our lives better, it makes sense to feel grateful. But when good things happen that make our lives better—and there's no intention behind it—it might make more sense to say we feel fortunate.

I feel grateful to medical researchers for finding treatments for terrible illnesses. I feel grateful to the mentors and colleagues who've helped me with my writing career. I feel grateful to Ingrid for almost everything she does every day.

But I feel fortunate to have been born with reasonably good health. I feel fortunate to live in reasonable comfort and security at a time of widespread economic distress. I feel wildly, astronomically fortunate to have been born at all.

I feel grateful to people. I feel fortunate for good luck.

There are places where these feelings of gratitude and good fortune overlap. I feel grateful to scientists who discovered treatments for illnesses—and fortunate to live in a time and place where these treatments are available. I feel grateful to people who have fought sexism and homophobia—and fortunate to live in a time and place where women and queers are treated with something vaguely resembling equality and respect. I feel grateful to Ingrid for almost everything she does every day—and fortunate for the fact that we met.

So it's not always an easy distinction to make. But it's useful. And this concept of good fortune preserves the moral and social value inherent in the concept of gratitude. When I feel fortunate, I don't feel churlish, entitled, or self-absorbed. I feel the same appreciation, the same obligation and urge to balance the scales, that I do when I feel grateful. When I'm conscious of how lucky I am—when I'm conscious of how much of the good stuff in my life landed in my lap without me earning it—it makes me appreciate my life, and inspires me to make the most of it. It makes me want to pay it forward. And it makes me want to help others who didn't get the breaks I got.

CHAPTER FIFTY-FOUR

Trekkie Religion and Secular Judaism: How Do We Use the Good Stuff from Religion?

How can atheists take the good stuff from religion and work it into our lives?

One of the most common tropes among believers is Religion As Metaphor: the idea that religious beliefs don't have to be literally true, they're just stories that give shape and meaning to our lives. I'm not buying it. If religion is just a story, why does it upset people so much when atheists say it isn't true? I think the metaphor trope is just a disingenuous way for believers to dodge hard questions. But it's got me thinking: If religions really were just stories—stories people found comforting and inspiring, that people knew weren't true but still enjoyed telling—what would that look like?

I once had a debate with a believer who got bent out of shape about how religion was just a comforting story. Religion could make a difference in people's lives, he insisted, without their belief in its literal truth—so why was I being mean and intolerant and trying to take it away? And it struck me: The version of religion he was talking about? It's Trekkies.

Think about it. Trekkies are devoted to a story they find entertaining and inspiring but that they know isn't factually real. And there's great diversity in their devotions, much like the diversity in religious beliefs.

Some Trekkies are intensely dedicated to the story, to the point where it takes up a substantial portion of their lives—going to conventions, making costumes, buying memorabilia, watching the shows again and again. Others are more casual followers, watching when *Star Trek* happens to be on, maybe taking in a convention or two. And different Trekkies follow different variants of the story. Some are more interested in the original series with Spock and Kirk; others care more about *The Next Generation*. Some weirdo fringe cultists even follow *Enterprise*.

But they know *Star Trek* isn't real. They know the story they're devoted to was made up by people. And they act accordingly. Avid convention-goers don't treat casual fans as ungodly; Original Seriesers don't treat Next Generationists as heretics; and none of them write editorials lambasting people as immoral sociopaths if they prefer documentaries to science fiction. And they don't insist that *Star Trek* is just a story—and then get bent out of shape when people point out that it's a story and therefore isn't true. Trekkies have a good time trying to fit the inaccuracies and inconsistencies into some sort of continuity (that's half the fun); but they understand that the show is a fictional story, with all the flaws that fiction is heir to, and they don't treat it as a perfect, divinely inspired guide to reality.

That's what religion would look like if it were just a metaphor. And if it looked like that, I would have no problem with it.

If you're a believer, you might think this analogy trivializes your faith. You might think it's insulting to compare centuries of serious practice and thought to nerds wearing Spock ears at convention centers. So let's take a different example—historical fiction re-creators, acting out the characters and worlds of Dickens, Shakespeare, F. Scott Fitzgerald, Jane Austen. Let's take communities who find these stories beautiful and inspiring, and devote significant portions of their lives to reading, studying, discussing and reimagining them, dressing up like characters from them, attending rituals and celebrations dedicated to them.

You don't like that analogy either? Well, that kind of proves my point. If believers get offended at their religion being compared to other stories—even serious literature—the trope that religion is just a story can't be sincere.

So if Trekkies are what religion would look like as a metaphor, are there any real religions being practiced that way?

Let's look at secular Judaism.

For many Jews, Judaism is entirely a cultural, historical, and familial identity, and not a religious one at all. The phrase "atheist Jew" has a non-absurd, readily comprehensible meaning, in a way that "atheist Baptist" doesn't. Many Jews cherrypick the rituals and stories they like and reject the ones they don't—not as a slippery way of trying to shoehorn an obsolete and untenable faith into a modern worldview, but openly and without shame or pretense, in an approach that says, "I don't think God gives a damn about this, I don't think God exists, this is all just mangled history and made-up mythology, so I have no qualms picking the parts I like and ditching the rest." Questioning the tenets of Judaism is part of the rabbinical tradition, and many secular Jews view their selective observance, not as a rejection of Jewish tradition, but as part of it. They treat sacred Jewish texts the way we all treat philosophers and political writers who aren't supposedly passing on the word of God: they read them critically, embrace the ideas that make sense, oppose the ones that are vile, and ignore the ones that seem silly.

Exactly the way *Star Trek* fans ignore and reject "Spock's Brain."

I guess I'm saying secular Jews are the Trekkies of religion. They treat the religion as a story: a fascinating story with a powerful tradition behind it, worth telling and caring about and getting involved in, but a story, with parts that are inspiring and useful, parts that are gruesome and ugly, and parts that are flat-out ridiculous.

There is, of course, an important difference between secular Judaism and Trekkies—the deep, intense connection many secular Jews have with family and history. For them, being a Jew isn't just about being invested in the stories and rituals. It's about the fact that their parents and grandparents and great-grandparents were invested in them too. And much of that investment has to do with how Jews and Judaism have historically been treated by the world. As a friend pointed out when I ran this piece by her: Plenty of Jews in Germany were very secular, and didn't particularly think of themselves as Jewish—but that didn't change how the Nazis saw them. Practicing the rituals of Judaism is a way of acknowledging this reality, of defying it, of saying "Fuck you" to Nazis, pogroms, ghettos, forced conversions, to the Protocols of the Elders of Zion, to being barred from all professions except money-lending and then vilified as money-grubbing usurers, to expulsions and massacres, the blood libel, the Spanish Inquisition. Secular Judaism isn't just about the fact that your great-grandmother practiced these rituals. It's about the fact that she was put in a concentration camp because of them.

So that's an important difference from Trekkies. But my basic premise remains. Secular Judaism is a way of preserving religious tradition without believing in God or the supernatural. Secular Judaism shows that you can take religious observances seriously, as a connection to family and history, without believing you're doing it for God. Judaism isn't alone in this, either. I'm beginning to hear of cultural Catholics following this pattern: they think the rituals and images are beautiful, an important part of their family history, but they don't actually believe it.

And you know what? I love this.

I would love to see more. I would love to see a secular Catholicism that preserves the soothing ritual and rich pageantry, without the sex-hating dogma and authoritarian hierarchy. I would love to see a secular Baptism that preserves the wild oratory and soaring music, without the hateful obsession with hellfire and judgment. I would love to see a secular Hinduism that preserves the magnificent imagery and generous diversity, without the rationalization for the caste system. I would love to see a secular Wicca that preserves the passionate love of nature, without the dismissive contempt for science that is so at odds with that love.

I probably wouldn't practice any of this myself. My own family's tradition is boring Midwestern Protestantism from my grandparents, and atheism from my parents. The former isn't interesting enough for me to preserve, and the latter I'm already running with. But I could totally see this as a way for humanity to preserve the cool stuff about religion—ritual and tradition, narrative and imagery, community and connection with family and history—without the active disregard for reality that causes so much trouble. And as an atheist, I could be totally happy with it.

So what's the difference between this secular Trekkie Judaism that I respect, the secular Trekkie Catholicism I'm encouraging—and the "Religion is a useful metaphor" trope that drives me up a tree?

The difference is this: Progressive believers say their religion is just a story—but they aren't sincere. You can tell by how bent out of shape they get when people point out that it's a story and therefore isn't true. They use the "metaphor" trope as a slippery way of avoiding hard questions from skeptics—but as soon as the skeptics are gone, they slip right back into real, non-metaphorical belief in the supernatural.

Truly secular practitioners, on the other hand, say, "This is just a story"—and mean it.

If you tell a "Religion is a metaphor" believer that their religion is a story, that it isn't factually true, that much of the history is mangled and some of it's flatly wrong, and that all the God stuff is totally made up—chances are they're going to get seriously defensive. They'll tell you how intolerant you are, how you're just as dogmatic and proselytizing as any fundamentalist, how disrespectful you are to point out the flaws in religion and try to persuade people that it's mistaken, how closed-minded you are to reject ideas just because they're not supported by facts.

If you say to a secular Jew, "Your religion is a story, it isn't factually true, a lot of the history is mangled and some of it's flatly wrong, and all the God stuff is totally made up"—chances are they'll say, "Yeah. I know. So are you coming to Passover or not?"

CHAPTER FIFTY-FIVE

For No Good Reason

Most people don't connect Morris dancing with transcendence. Most people who have seen Morris dancing connect it with cacophony, silly outfits, and beer. But I had this moment of atheist transcendence at the Black And White Morris Tour, and it got me thinking about why we do the things we do.

A quick bit of background. Morris dancing is a more or less harmless enterprise that involves dressing in colorful outfits and dancing in smallish groups, strapping bells to your legs, clashing sticks together or waving hankies about. It's an English folk tradition, and while many Morris dancers will tell entertaining lies about how incredibly ancient it is, it's actually about 500 years old. My darling wife Ingrid is deeply involved with it, but I love her anyway.

A Morris outing usually involves one or more teams each dressing in their own team outfits, with each team performing their own dances. The Black and White Tour is different. Everyone dresses in whatever combination of black and white strikes their fancy, and the dances are common ones that many dancers know, so just about everyone can do them all.

It was magnificent.

I don't dance the Morris myself anymore. I was just there to watch and hoot. And I was gobsmacked. I've seen a lot of Morris dancing in my life—Ingrid's done it for years, and I did it for years before she did—and while I enjoy it, I've seen enough to last several lifetimes, and I'm not easily impressed. This time, I was more than impressed. I had my breath taken away. It was one of the most beautiful, memorable things I've ever seen.

And it was all for no good reason.

Which brings me back to atheism, and atheist transcendence.

It's hard to describe what exactly made this day so breathtaking. Part of it was the beautiful blend of individual expression and group coherence. So much of life stresses one at the expense of the other. The Black and White tour hit that rare, perfect balance between the two—the joy of working together, and the joy of being yourself. The outfits were a perfect example: the vision was specific enough to create a coherent look, while allowing great room for individuality. And the fact that the performances were mish-moshes of people who rarely danced together added to the goofy, boisterous glee. It wasn't about precision. It was about joy.

And partly it was just beautiful—the black and white of the dancers capering in the sunlight, set against the Victorian white wood and glass of the Conservatory of Flowers and the green, green grass of Golden Gate Park. It looked like some wild, arty circus had come to town.

But much of what made it so magnificent was the sheer, beautiful absurdity.

There is no good reason on earth to do Morris dancing. It is an utterly pointless activity. Sure, you get some exercise and social contact, but you can get social contact lots of places, and you get better exercise at the gym. It isn't constructive; it isn't important; it doesn't produce anything. All it produces is joy.

If you're an atheist, that's what life is like.

There's no purpose or meaning other than what we create. In a few decades we're all going to be gone, dust in the ground or ashes in the wind. In a few billion years the earth and everything on it will be gone, boiled away into the sun; in a few more billion years, the universe will be gone, dissipated into a thin scattering of atoms dotted through vast stretches of emptiness. There's no light at the end of the tunnel, no final chapter that ties up all the loose ends. And there's no big daddy in the sky to shake your hand at the end and say, "You done good, kid. Here's your gold star."

And yet—here we are. We were, against wildly astronomical odds, born. The odds of any one of us being alive are so slim as to be a joke. No, there's no purpose to it, if purpose means being a cog in someone else's machine. There's no reason for it to have happened—except that it did. The only meaning is whatever meaning we create.

We can do that in our work. We can do it in our art. We can do it in our friendships, our relationships, our families. We can do it in politics, charities, community involvement, social justice work. We can do it with cooking. We can do it with fashion. We can do it with sex. And we can do it by dressing in ridiculous outfits, strapping bells to our legs, and dancing in the park like fools.

CHAPTER FIFTY-SIX

Imposter Syndrome, and What It Means to Be an Adult

"I don't feel like an adult."

Does this sound familiar? "My adult life looks nothing like I thought it would. I thought I'd have it together by now. I thought by now, I'd be finished with school, be married, have kids, have a stable job. Sure, I'm doing (insert list of awesome, inspiring, difficult things)—but I can't balance my checkbook, I do my laundry at the last minute, I eat like a teenager, I'm scrambling for money at the end of every month, I have eight thousand unanswered emails, I clean my house for parties by shoving all my junk into grocery bags and piling them in the closet. What's wrong with me?"

I know so many people who feel this way. In fact, I'd be hard-pressed to think of an adult in my life who doesn't feel this way, at least to some degree. So I started wondering: What's up with that?

Many religions have coming-of-age traditions, rites of passage in which children declare themselves to finally be adults. Many non-believers are doing our own non-religious versions, such as baby namings and coming-of-age ceremonies. I think this is a fine idea. But lots of non-believers don't have these rituals. So I think it's worth considering: How do we define adulthood? And how do we know when we've gotten there?

As non-religious people, we reject the religious definitions of adulthood. For one thing, religious coming-of-age traditions are often less about real adulthood, and more about declaring yourself an adult so you can make a supposedly adult commitment to your faith. And as freethinkers, we're more likely to reject the standard set of cultural markers, such as the idea that adulthood equals marriage, financial stability, higher education, and so on. If we reject these standard definitions, what does adulthood mean—and why do so many of us have a hard time laying claim to it?

You may have heard of imposter syndrome, the tendency of accomplished people to see themselves as frauds who don't deserve success or recognition, despite significant evidence to the contrary. People with imposter syndrome discount their successes, attribute their success to luck, fear being found out and exposed, and assume that everyone else is more talented and organized than they are. I think imposter syndrome can apply to more than just career accomplishments. I think it can apply to life, and our ability to navigate it.

A big part of this, I think, comes from how we see adulthood when we're growing up. As kids, we tend to see adults as infallible, omniscient, having everything figured out. But once we're adults, we see how fallible we are and how much we're making things up as we go along—so we feel like failures. Or at least, we don't feel like grownups. (I sometimes wonder if this feeds the religious impulse. The panicked realization that you don't really know what you're doing, and nobody else knows what they're doing, and nobody is driving the bus—it could easily make people yearn for an all-knowing, all-powerful Parent in the Sky who actually does have things under control.)

It's also easy to focus on our failures rather than our successes. This is understandable: humans are problem solvers, and if we're trying to make things better, it's easy to focus on what isn't working. But it does lead to dissatisfaction. It's easy to have "grass is greener" syndrome when we're assessing our lives. It's easy to see other people's lives as more together than ours, since that's the face people usually present. As a friend said when we were talking about this, "Keep in mind you only see the side of other people's lives that they want you to see. Sort of like when you think everyone has a clean place but you. They cleaned it because you were coming over!"

And seeing ourselves as adults can be especially hard for people with unconventional careers and lives. Our culture's idea of what it means to be an adult can be somewhat rigid—marriage, kids, nice home, stable job. In my head, I know this is crap: there are countless adults I admire and am inspired by whose lives look nothing like that. I know people who left high-paying career tracks to do relief work; who dropped out of school to become artists or musicians or writers; who went to school to pursue uncertain careers in social work or health care or something else they think matters, instead of going for the big bucks; who rejected monogamous marriage and are inventing relationship structures that work for them. But that rigid view of adulthood is everywhere, and it's hard not to buy into. And when you're carving out your own life, by definition there's no cultural template; no yardstick to measure yourself against and decide if you're doing okay.

Yet that very lack of a template may point the way out of this trap. I'm not sure I could come up with a simple, soundbite definition of adulthood. But if I had to, it would probably be "carving out your own life." It wouldn't have anything to do with one particular marker. It would be about deciding which markers matter to you—and doing what's necessary to make them happen. It would be about taking responsibility for your choices, and accepting the consequences.

Adulthood isn't about any particular signpost. It means painting the signs yourself.

And there are advantages to letting go of this fantasy of perfect adulthood, where we're always secure and consistent and sensible, with smooth-running lives that never get blindsided. Positive Flip-side

Number One: Most of us have a poor understanding of what makes us happy. We tend to think happiness means letting go of work and responsibility, lazing on a beach with a margarita in our hand. Nope. That's good for a while, but we soon get bored and restless. What actually makes most people happy is working on a task we care about, one that's challenging but within our capability. This fantasy of a perfect adulthood where there's nothing left to do? BOR-ing.

Positive Flip-side Number Two: A life that can blindside you is a life that can surprise you. And I want surprises. I want to pull into a diner in a strange town and have the best bread I've ever eaten. I want to wander into a shoe store on a whim and decide that yes, despite years of resisting the idea, I am falling in love with those four-inch stiletto pumps. I want to go see a band my friend's co-worker is in, and be transfixed and transported, to the point where I continue to follow them for the next fifteen years. I want to go on a date for what's supposed to be a casual holiday fling, and two weeks later call her to tell her I love her, and five years later ask her to marry me, and eighteen years later still be wildly in love with her.

Sure, part of me wants everything to run smoothly. But when I think carefully about what that would look like, it makes me want to run screaming for the exits. It's like Heaven: I can't imagine any version of it in which I would be myself, yet somehow not be bored to the point of despair. If I want a life that can surprise me, I have to take the bad surprises with the good.

And finally, Positive Flip-side Number Three:

I once read that for many people in my generation, and in the generations after mine, we've been re-defining adulthood as playtime. We see adulthood not as the time when we automatically get slotted into marriage, parenthood, and a stable career we stick with until we retire, but as the time when we can choose for ourselves what's important to us. And if part of what we want to do is go rock-climbing, sing karaoke, play Grand Theft Auto, drink ridiculous cocktails, or dress up in corsets and stockings and go to the Edward Gorey ball—we get to do that.

Of course we have to make the choices that let us do these things; hold down a job, pay our bills, etc. But adulthood means the freedom to set these priorities for ourselves. We get to decide whether we'd rather have clean laundry or watch *America's Best Dance Crew*; whether we'd rather eat chocolate cake for dinner every night or lose twenty pounds; whether we care more about traveling across the country or saving money to buy a house; whether we want to keep that comfortable well-paying job or live on beans and rice for a few years while we try to make it as an artist.

And that is awesome.

I don't remember where I first heard this, but I've seen responsibility defined as accepting the degree to which we are the cause of our lives. That can be hard: it means when things go south, we have to accept, at least sometimes, that our behavior is part of what made that happen. But there's a side of responsibility that's awesome. It means our lives are our own. We tend to hear the word "responsibility" and think it means burden, blame, or being boring and always making the safe choice. But it can also mean freedom—the freedom to make our own choices, and to use them to shape our lives.

Adulthood doesn't mean freedom from responsibility. It means the freedom *of* responsibility. And responsibility doesn't mean having your shit perfectly together. That's not an option, and we wouldn't want it if it were. Letting go of that expectation is hard and unsettling. But it's also liberating, and it has the capacity to make us genuinely happy.

Yes, I sometimes feel like a failure as a grown-up because I have money worries; because I let things slip through the cracks; because I get overwhelmed and freaked out by all the stuff I have to take care of; because I sometimes make bad choices I know are bad even as I'm making them; because my life isn't perfectly protected from a monkey wrench sailing in from out of nowhere and grinding the gears to a halt;

because I sometimes blow off my responsibilities and watch *What Not to Wear* instead. And yes, when I was growing up, I saw adulthood as secure and sensible and having everything figured out. But I also saw it as boring, joyless, dour, predictable, and trapped. And I am so glad to be wrong about that.

Accepting without question the cultural standards of adulthood, doing what everyone expects of you simply because they expect it—that's the opposite of responsible. That's the opposite of adult. But if you do what matters to you, and accept the burdens and consequences and risks of that choice—in my eyes, you are an adult.

CHAPTER FIFTY-SEVEN

Work/Life Balance

My two hands are not getting along.

On the one hand, the purpose of a humanist life is to make the world better. On the other hand, the purpose of a humanist life is to experience the world as richly and fully as possible. There are times when these hands work together, peacefully and efficiently, each complementing the other, and each growing stronger and more dexterous from the other's support. Taking pleasure in my life gives me the mental and emotional nourishment to carry on with my work. Doing productive work makes it easier to take pleasure from the world, knowing I've made a contribution to it, and feeling a deep connection with it. At times, the two are indistinguishable: the work itself is a deep, replenishing pleasure, something I would totally do even if I had no responsibilities to uphold and weren't being paid.

Then there are times when these two hands battle like mortal enemies. At the best of those times, it's like having a thumb war with myself; at the worst, it's like one hand is viciously attacking the other, wrenching it at the wrist and trying to choke the life out of it. Usually, it's the work hand trying to destroy the life hand.

I recently took up drawing as a hobby. I've been having some difficult struggles with depression, and I thought—correctly, as it turned out—that drawing would be an easy, low-investment, mentally healthy way to keep my mind engaged, and to keep from fixating on upsetting things I can't change.

Why drawing? For pretty much my whole life, I've been fairly good at visual arts, but not mega-awesome or in any way ambitious. You might think it's weird to take up a hobby I'm not mega-awesome at—but that's a big part of the point. I want a hobby I don't have to be self-critical or goal-oriented about, something that isn't for public consumption, something purely for my own enjoyment. If I want to draw my backyard, or geometric patterns, or elaborate scenes of a happy monster society that makes sense to no-one but me—I can do that. If an image isn't recognizable to anyone but me, or doesn't turn out how I intended, I can enjoy where it wound up, or shrug and turn the page and do something else. And I can take pleasure from the physical process, the sensual flow of pencil on paper. I can draw based entirely on where it feels good to put the pencil, which hand movements make my brain feel good. Interwoven spirals? Fountains of feathery strokes? Pages of graph paper painstakingly filled with colored-in squares? Why not?

At the same time, I'm noticing how difficult it is to keep doing this purely for my own sake. I'm noticing how deep a habit it is to be goal-oriented and self-critical, to get irritated with my mistakes, to get excited if I seem to be getting better or frustrated if I feel like I'm getting worse. (Better or worse at what? At enjoying myself?) And I'm noticing the urge to post the art on my blog or on Facebook. I've decided not to for the time being: if I knew I'd be posting the artwork online, I'd be stressing about what other people thought, and I'd be missing the whole point. But I'm tempted to do it almost every day.

See, without making the drawings part of my public work, it's hard not to think of them as a waste of time. It's hard to look ahead ten years, imagine a file cabinet filled with notebooks of drawings nobody sees but me—and not think of all the things I could be accomplishing instead with that time. Even here, I introduced my drawings as a form of mental health care. They are—but why did I need to defend my hobby by defining it as medicine? Why did I need to defend it at all?

U.S. culture is obsessed with work, and tends to see time off as a sign of laziness, selfishness, and lack of ambition. Our views on work and pleasure are rooted in Puritanism, and its notions that our bodies are disgusting fonts of sin, that the world is a festering swamp of temptation, and that the purpose of our lives is to do God's work and get our sinful asses to Heaven. My screwed-up views on work/life balance didn't spring up in a vacuum. But it's up to me to push back.

There's a talk I give on preventing and treating burnout, and one of the key pieces of advice is to get a hobby; to get a life outside work or activism, and do things purely to nourish yourself. One of the points I make is that if we want to keep producing work, we need to give ourselves self-care. I tell my audience to think of themselves as a fruit tree or a car. If we want the tree to bear fruit, we need water and sunlight. If we want the car to move forward, we need gas and maintenance. If we want to keep working, we have to replenish ourselves.

It's good advice. But it doesn't go far enough. Balancing work and life doesn't mean giving ourselves the bare minimum of self-care, just enough to grease the engines of activism and ambition. It isn't about watering the tree so the tree can bear fruit for other people. It's about watering the tree so the tree can live a satisfying tree life. Yes, as humanists, we should be driven by compassion. But the targets of our compassion should include ourselves. A work/life balance means you get to have a life.

CHAPTER FIFTY-EIGHT

"Ya Gotta Reach for Your Dreams"

Should we, in fact, always reach for our dreams?

You've seen the movies, the TV shows; you've read the inspiring books. Scrappy underdog with a dream struggles against all odds to astonish everyone and win the big game at the end. It's the *Flashdance/Bend It Like Beckham/Mighty Ducks* trope, deeply embedded in our culture. You can do anything you want, if you set your mind to it. Take your passion, and make it happen.

In my ongoing attempt to be both an optimist and a realist, I've been thinking about this trope—and I want to take it on. Yes, it's often good to reach for our dreams. But I hate this trope, and I think it does real damage. It undercuts a realistic view of the world, and in a weird way, it undercuts optimism.

If you try hard enough, you'll succeed. That's what the trope strongly implies, and even promises outright. But if you look at the world for ten minutes, you'll see this is patently untrue. Not everyone reaches their dreams. The world is full of singers who never get on the radio; athletes who never make it past college; students who flunk out of med school; writers who never write a bestseller or never get published at all.

It isn't always for lack of trying. Sometimes it's for lack of talent. The *American Idol* tryouts are Exhibit A. They're a sad parade of self-deception; a nearly endless caravan of dreadful singers who saw *Flashdance* and *The Mighty Ducks* and think this is their shot, that if they work hard and stay true to their dream they'll someday be a star. The line between confidence and a fool's paradise is a tricky one.

And sometimes failure is simply for lack of luck. As any successful person who isn't totally arrogant will tell you, luck plays a huge role in success. That's especially true in difficult, highly competitive fields. You have to be talented, ambitious, a hard worker—*and* you have to get the breaks. And the often-overlooked breaks of birth and upbringing are some of the biggest.

Hard work and determination are no guarantee of success. And some of the hardest lessons to learn, some of the hardest choices to make, are when to keep trying and when to let go; which setbacks are just obstacles on your path to glory, and which ones are the universe telling you it ain't gonna happen. This isn't just about careers, either. I've hung onto relationships that were dead and rotting because I was convinced that if we tried hard enough we could make it work.

These are some of our hardest, most wrenching decisions. And this trope, the notion that you'll win in the end if you stick to your dreams, can cloud our thinking about them. It can make people think their big break is just around the corner, that they can't give up now, that if they just stick with it long enough it's bound to happen.

Besides, not everyone has security enough to reach for their dreams, or opportunity enough to have a decent chance of realizing them. Some people can drop everything to become a tree surgeon, and the worst thing that will happen is they'll crash on their friend's couch for a few months while they find another job as a software engineer. For others, the worst things that can happen are poverty, permanent debt, the cycle of poverty, loss of child custody, homelessness. Dreams don't have to be career dreams, of course—they can be about art, travel, politics, sports, almost any area of our lives. But when they are about career, they have the power to seriously alter a life. They're decisions we need to think about carefully—and that's harder to do when there's a chorus of Hollywood screenwriters in our ears chanting, "Go for it!"

And when people don't succeed, this trope can make them feel even worse. This is what I mean about undercutting optimism. If you already feel bad about failing, you now feel like a double failure because you gave up. You're convinced that if you'd really wanted it badly enough, if you'd worked harder or had more confidence or stuck it out just a little longer, you'd be on your way to dreamtown. How much harder will it be to pursue your next dream, if you start out feeling like your last failure is proof of a character flaw?

You shouldn't reach for your dreams because sooner or later, with enough confidence and hard work, you'll succeed.

You should reach for your dreams if you can because you may or may not succeed if you try—but you sure as hell won't succeed if you don't. Because reaching itself can get you to places that are interesting and worthwhile, even if they're not where you originally set out to go. Because reaching can be satisfying and valuable, regardless of where it takes you. Because you'll regret it if you don't.

And you should reach for your dreams because—well, what else are you going to do? You have one life. Are you going to spend it trying to do what matters to you, or wondering what would have happened if you had?

When you're near the end of your life, would you rather look back and say, "Boy, I wish I'd tried to be a tree surgeon. I bet I would have been really good at it. I guess now I'll never know"? Or would you rather look back and say, "What a life I've had! Look at all the wild things I did. Remember when I was in that mini-golf championship? Remember when I tried to grow sweet potatoes in the bathtub? Remember when I tried to be a tree surgeon? Boy, did that ever not work out—but it sure was interesting to try."

CHAPTER FIFTY-NINE

Letting the World Surprise You

It was Halloween. One of Ingrid's Morris dance teams had a practice scheduled, so they decided to do some ad hoc performances in public. I tagged along: I didn't think it'd be anything special, but I like her teammates, I didn't have anything else planned, and I wanted to hang out with Ingrid on Halloween.

It was astonishing.

The first dance was at the USS Hornet, the aircraft carrier that recovered the astronauts from the Apollo 11 and 12 moon landings, and which is now a national historic landmark. (They were doing night tours for Halloween.) It's a massive, weirdly beautiful object, spooky and particularly imposing at night. And the dancing in front of it was one of the strangest, most beautiful sights I've seen. The outfits for this team were both festive and dark, with rag coats in blacks and grays, and top hats with black veils. Even in broad daylight they can look eerie and slightly menacing: here, they were unearthly.

And I watched, snapping pictures and just standing there agog at how gorgeous and bizarre and unexpected it was. Out of all the odd turns my life could have taken, watching my wife's Morris dance troupe perform at an aircraft carrier on Halloween night had to be high up on the list. And not just any aircraft carrier—the one that picked up the Apollo astronauts!

Their second dance was in front of a movie theater—a less unusual space, but more of an audience. I watched the onlookers as much as the dancing, and got to experience their surprise and delight; passers-by on their way to the next trick-or-treat stop, happily interrupted by veiled folk dancers in rag coats dancing to accordion music in front of the theater. There were little kids with huge eyes; parents grinning at their kids; grownups snapping a hundred pictures; teenagers capering alongside and cracking up, semi-mocking but also appreciating the spirit, wanting to join in. There was one kid, about thirteen, who stopped dead on the street when the music started, and stood stock still, jaw hanging open, mesmerized. His older sister (I'm guessing) kept trying to move him along—and he would not budge. He was going to see as much of this as he could.

There is so much in this life I've never seen. I want to see as much of it as I can.

When I became an atheist, one of the biggest changes was how much more open to the world I became—and how much more I was willing to be surprised by it. When I chose to prioritize reality over whatever pre-existing opinions I might have about it, and when I made this a conscious philosophy and guiding principle, my life opened up in ways I couldn't have imagined. It's opened up in large ways, like flying around the country giving talks to crowds of strangers, and having a large number of friends and colleagues who are young enough to be my kids. It's opened up in small ways, like taking time to absorb the street art in my neighborhood, and stopping at a food cart to buy a coconut curry ice cream pop. I feel an excitement about my life that I didn't have before; this incredible sense of good fortune about the fact that there's a universe, and that I get to be alive in it. And I feel this sense of urgency, almost responsibility, to not let myself get world-weary and jaded, and to let myself be gobsmacked.

Of course life had surprises before I became an atheist. But I feel much more intimately connected with the universe now that I'm not lying to myself about it. And I feel more capable of being astonished by it. Like I said at the start of this book: Our world gets bigger when we let reality in. It gets bigger when we let reality take priority over whatever ideas we might have about it. Reality is bigger than we are. Our world gets bigger when we let reality be what it is—and when we pay attention to it, as carefully we can.

There is a sadness to this sometimes. It can be intensely frustrating to know there are restaurants I'll never eat at, movies I'll never see, books I'll never read, people I'll never meet. But that makes me even more passionate about the restaurants and movies and books and people that *are* in my life. It makes me feel more driven to stay present with them, to not space out and drift into my own little world, to connect with them and see what surprises they might have in store. Sometimes these surprises are big and obvious—seeing Scotland for the first time, or speaking to a crowd of 20,000 people, or meeting someone out of the blue who within a year would be one of my best friends. And sometimes they're the small, subtle surprises of everyday life—the taste of scones from a new bakery, or some silly, wonderful video of a guy dancing in his rec room, or an afternoon with friends in a bland hotel conference room laughing ourselves into insensibility.

Or the sight of my wife's Morris team on Halloween night, dancing in black veils and dark rag coats in front of an aircraft carrier.

CHAPTER SIXTY

In Praise of Frivolity

When atheists consider the question of meaning without God, we often answer with The Big Things. Love, work, art, family. Marriage. Friendship. Making love. Community, charity work, making the world a better place, the never-ending search for knowledge. All of these are awesome; all of them are central parts of how I create meaning in my own life.

But I'd like to add a few items to that list. What brings meaning to my life? Donuts. Fashion magazines. Costume jewelry. Cat videos. Playing Zombie Fluxx. Pretentious overpriced cocktails with a lot of ridiculous crap in them. Dicking around on Facebook. TiVoing the Olympics and watching obscure sports we've never heard of. Cat videos. Coming up with a sexy, gorgeous, wildly inappropriate outfit for the Dyke March. Padron peppers sautéed in hot olive oil until they blister, then sprinkled with sea salt. Fucking. Sitting on the sofa watching *Project Runway* and letting cats crawl all over us. Cat videos. The never-ending search for a perfect cup of decaf coffee.

I want to speak in praise of frivolity.

When we don't think there's any god or afterlife, we can certainly create meaning from work and art, charity and activism, from children living after us, our ideas surviving us, the ripples of how we affect people continuing to ripple out after we're gone. But if other people are the meaning of our life, what meaning do *their* lives have? If we exist to make other people happy, and they exist to make still other people happy—at what point does that end?

At some point, doesn't experience get to just matter, simply because it matters?

Consciousness is amazing. All of it. The overflowing love I felt the day Ingrid and I got married was amazing—and the deliciousness I tasted this morning when I ate tangerines and drank coffee was amazing. The sense of accomplishment and community I felt the day I published my first book was amazing—and my hysterical, uncontrollable laughter when we were playing Zombie Fluxx at the hot chocolate and games party was amazing. The connection I felt with Rebecca and Gerard in our intense conversation about queer history was amazing—and the connection I felt with Ingrid in last night's ridiculous conversation about our cats was amazing.

The frivolous bits of life are the universe knowing itself, experiencing itself, and taking joy in itself. They're the conscious bits of the universe connecting with each other; through one person handing a cup of coffee across a counter and another person smiling and saying, "Thank you," through one person designing a hot pink dress and another person wearing it and smiling at their reflection in a window, through one person painting a picture of a parrot on the sidewalk and another person snapping a picture of it and putting it on their blog, through one person writing a silly song and another person sharing it with their friend and that friend humming it throughout their day, through one person taking a video of their cat and another person liking it on Facebook; through one person making a donut and another person biting into it and experiencing joy.

When we let go of the idea that life is only meaningful because of God, when we truly accept that meaning is ours to create, we can stop being size queens about meaning. When we let go of the idea that joy only matters when it brings glory to an omnipotent creator, we can let all joy matter.

CHAPTER SIXTY-ONE

Part of the Show

One last atheist epiphany before we go.

It was at the Edwardian Ball. That's not Edwardian as in King Edward VII, but as in the artist Edward Gorey, known for his finely detailed, hilariously ghoulish depictions of Victoriana, Edwardiana, and Roaring Twenties flapperdom. The Edwardian Ball started years ago as a little nightclub gig by the self-described pagan lounge band Rosin Coven, and has mushroomed into a massive, magnificent, weekend-long event, with live music, ballroom dancing, costumes, art, exhibitions, absinthe cocktails, trapeze performances, weird taxidermy displays, and more. It's where the Goth, steampunk, ballroom, and historical re-creation scenes collide in a magnificent explosion.

I love it passionately. It happens every year, and we never miss it if we can help it. It is a near-perfect example of what I think of as the atheist meaning of life.

When you don't believe in God or an afterlife—when you don't think the meaning of your life is determined by a divine force, and when you understand that humanity is just a tiny, fragile, absurdly mortal fragment in the immensity of space and time—you have to seriously rethink the whole question of what life means. The meaning of life isn't pleasing God and going to Heaven, or perfecting your soul for your next reincarnation, or working towards the enlightenment of the World-Soul. And humanity isn't a singularly beloved creation with a special destiny. We're just an unusually complex biochemical process on one small rock whizzing around one nondescript star in one of billions of galaxies. And when that star goes out in a few billion years, that biochemical process is destined to go out along with it, with no traces left but a few bits of space junk floating in the emptiness.

The Edwardian Ball looks at all this, and says, "Let's celebrate. And let's connect.

"Let's spend hours putting together magnificent outfits, so other people can look at them and go, 'Oooo!' Let's spend years learning and practicing and playing music, so other people can dance and be happy. Let's spend years learning and practicing and performing trapeze work and acrobatics, so other people can gaze in admiration. This is what we have to work with: the matter on this little planet, the energy from this average star, the tiny lifespan before each of us dies, the not-much-longer lifespan of the planet before humanity is boiled into space. What can we do with it? What are some of the strangest, funniest, most beautiful patterns we can work this matter and energy into before we have to go?"

The Edwardian Ball is one of my favorite examples of stone soup culture; of people who know the party will be more fun if they bring their share of it. It isn't just about hearing other people's music, watching other people's stage shows, looking at other people's art. Everywhere I looked, people were dressed to the nines: in rigorously accurate historical costumes, in fanciful imaginings of fictional history, in elegant formal dress, in irreverent and hilarious re-interpretations of formal dress, in complicated technological marvels, in artfully lascivious displays of flesh, in elaborate configurations of black on black on black. And people were dancing, creating a delightful whirlpool of giddy, ridiculous glamour whizzing around the dance floor. The audience was as much a part of the event as the performers. This event is not about sitting back passively and waiting to be entertained. It's about being part of the show.

When I'm in a despondent mood, I sometimes get depressed about the closed circle of human endeavor. I'm not naturally a Zen, "in the moment" person; I'm ambitious, forward thinking, and I like to think of my effect on the world as possibly having some life beyond my reach and extending past my death. It sometimes makes me sad to remember that, even if I mysteriously become the most famous and influential person in the history of the planet, it's still a closed circle—because life on Earth is a closed circle, and there's no god or world-soul to carry my thoughts and experiences into infinity. Like Roy Batty says at the end of *Bladerunner*: "All those moments will be lost in time, like tears in rain."

The Edwardian ball reminds me, "So what? So what if you're spending hours on your outfit just to be seen and admired by a couple thousand other people, whose outfits you're also admiring? So what if you're working to make life a skosh more joyful for people who'll be dead in a few decades anyway, and whose descendants will be boiled into the sun in a few billion years? Don't those people matter? Don't you matter? The odds against you being born at all were beyond astronomical. Beating your breast in despair because you're going to die is like winning a million dollars in the lottery and complaining that it wasn't a hundred trillion. You're here now, and these other people are here. Experience your life, and connect with theirs. Even if it's just to spend a moment admiring each other's marvelous outfits."

The Edwardian ball reminds me that permanence is not the only measure of consequence or value. The Edwardian ball reminds me that, fragile and transitory as they are, experience and consciousness are freaking miracles. And the fact that we can share experiences and connect our consciousnesses, even to the flawed and limited degree that we do, is beyond miraculous.

Let's be part of the show.

For me, as an atheist, the meaning of life is participation, connection, and joy. Sometimes that means staying up until four in the morning writing about atheism and sex. Sometimes it means singing the James K. Polk song to my friend's new baby. Sometimes it means doing copywriting and website maintenance for a hippie-anarchist-punk publishing house. Sometimes it means cramming twenty people into our apartment for a sit-down Christmas Eve dinner. Sometimes it means trying to make people give a damn about racism. Sometimes it means dutifully going to see our friend's co-worker's band, and becoming fans overnight. Sometimes it means donating money to earthquake relief in Haiti. Sometimes it means writing about the atheist meaning of life.

And sometimes it means dressing up like a character in an elegantly ghoulish fictional world, drinking absinthe cocktails, and waltzing the night away with my beloved wife, in a ballroom full of taxidermied animals and beautiful nerds who spent hours on their costumes.

I can live with that.

ACKNOWLEDGMENTS

First, last, and always: Ingrid.

I have so much to say about Alex Gabriel, but it boils down to this: If you're looking for a copy editor, hire him. He cares fiercely about the craft of writing, and discusses its broadest strokes and minutest details with thoughtfulness, precision, patience, and humor. (He is almost certainly irritated at that last comma.) He is a hardass in the best way: I can't count the number of times I reacted to his suggestion for a major restructuring or a huge cut with a flaming temper tantrum, and two hours later was excitedly typing and thinking, "He's right, he's a genius, it's so much better this way." And his suggestions were always made with a respect for my voice, and a desire for it to shine. He wanted this book to be the best it could possibly be, almost as much as I did, and occasionally more so. His ideas have made me rethink some of my basic approaches to writing, always for the better. And he will spend ridiculous amounts of time passionately debating whether grass is green, or the linguistics, style, and philosophy of the word "that." The book is far better because of his work on it—and working with him is a joy.

When Ingrid and I started dating, I'm not sure she realized what she was signing on for. She has had countless pieces of writing dumped in her lap, from blog posts to entire books, with pleading requests for feedback, proofreading, and approval. For this book in particular, she spent hours of her spare time, a rare commodity in her life, copy editing and proofreading the manuscript. She listened to me gas on about it for hours more. And she put up with my mood swings, my distraction, the mornings I didn't come to bed until she was getting up. If I were going to come up with a creative curse, it might be, "May you always be married to a writer in the last month before their book deadline." If I believed in saints, I would say Ingrid has the patience of one. For better and for worse, sweetie. I still do.

If anyone wants some compelling, entertaining, thought-provoking, and hilarious conversation about atheism, religion, sex, gender, skepticism, science, social justice, pop culture, and the places where all these overlap, The Godless Perverts Social Club is a unique and extraordinary resource. Many of the ideas in this book were sparked or developed there. I want to thank everyone who's come to a meetup and asked questions, told stories, or thought out loud. I especially want to thank the regulars and volunteers, who do this month after month. And I especially, double especially, ten times especially, want to thank Chris Hall, co-founder and co-organizer of Godless Perverts, and my dear friend and partner in crime.

Everything I just said also applies to Freethought Blogs and my colleagues there. The years I've blogged there have changed my life, and have made my career as an atheist writer. And I'm hugely grateful to my blog readers for challenging me, supporting me, and understanding that you can do both.

And I am beyond grateful to my colleagues at my new blog home, The Orbit. Starting a business at the same time I was writing a book was absurd beyond measure, but creating this site with all of you has been one of the great challenges and joys of my life. I am so happy to be working with such a talented, committed, passionate, principled group, and I'm so excited to see what we're going to do!

Did I mention Ingrid? Ingrid. For better or for worse, in sickness and in health, in conflict and tranquility, in poverty and in comfort. I have never doubted that she is on my side and that we are on the same team.

Many thanks to my editors and publishers at AlterNet, Blowfish, Free Inquiry, and The Humanist. Many of the chapters in this book were originally published in these publications: they gave me space to explore these ideas, and money so I could keep doing it.

Of all the compliments I've gotten about my books over the years, one of the most consistent is, "The cover art is amazing!" Meeting Casimir Fornalski is one of the best pieces of luck in my writing career.

There are probably dozens of people I need to thank and can't. If I ever had a conversation with you about atheism, and you weren't a flaming asshole, your ideas shaped my thinking. If you're one of the people I've had dozens of conversations with, your friendship helped make this movement a home.

Pitchstone Publishing has given me guidance on where to go, latitude to go there, a platform to fire off from, and fuel to stoke the fires. I love writing for them.

And last, first, and always: Ingrid.

RESOURCE GUIDE

There are a lot of resources available to atheists: this is by no means an exhaustive list. It's just meant to get you started. The focus is on resources that support living a good atheist life, and on gateways that can point you to other resources. A more comprehensive resource guide is available in *Coming Out Atheist: How to Do It, How to Help Each Other, and Why*: it's also available on my blog, at the-orbit.net/greta.

ORGANIZATIONS/ COMMUNITIES/ SUPPORT GROUPS

African Americans for Humanism
Supports skeptics, doubters, humanists, and atheists in the African American community, provides forums for communication and education, and facilitates coordinated action to achieve shared objectives.
aahumanism.net

American Atheists
Working for the civil liberties of atheists and the total, absolute separation of government and religion.
atheists.org

American Humanist Association
Advocating progressive values and equality for humanists, atheists, and freethinkers.
americanhumanist.org

Atheist Alliance International
A global federation of atheist and freethought groups and individuals, committed to educating its members and the public about atheism, secularism and related issues.
atheistalliance.org

Black Nonbelievers
Walking by sight, not by faith. A non-profit fellowship of nonbelievers dedicated to providing informative, caring, festive and friendly environments for Blacks and their allies. A national organization with local affiilate groups around the United States.
blacknonbelievers.wordpress.com

British Humanist Association
They work on behalf of non-religious people who seek to live ethical lives on the basis of reason and humanity. They promote Humanism, a secular state, and equal treatment of everyone regardless of religion or belief.
humanism.org.uk

Camp Quest
Residential summer camps that provide an educational adventure shaped by fun, friends and freethought, featuring science, natural wonder and humanist values.
campquest.org

Center for Inquiry
Their mission is to foster a secular society based on science, reason, freedom of inquiry, and humanist values. They have many local branches with regular meetings.
centerforinquiry.net

The Clergy Project
A confidential online community for current and former religious professionals without supernatural beliefs.
clergyproject.org

Council of Australian Humanist Societies
Umbrella organization for humanist societies around Australia.
humanist.org.au

Council of Ex-Muslims of Britain
Nonbelievers, atheists, and ex-Muslims are establishing or joining the Council of Ex-Muslims of Britain to insist that no one be pigeonholed as Muslims with culturally relative rights nor deemed to be represented by regressive Islamic organisations and "Muslim community leaders."
ex-muslim.org.uk

Ex-Muslims of North America
An organization dedicated to supporting and helping Ex-Muslims. They aim to build a community and provide a sense of solidarity for "Ex-Muslims"—people who used to follow Islam or identify as Muslim, and who no longer do so.
exmna.org

Filipino Freethinkers
The largest and most active group of non-believers and progressive believers in the Philippines.
filipinofreethinkers.org

Foundation Beyond Belief
A charitable foundation created to demonstrate humanism at its best by supporting efforts to improve this world and this life, and to challenge humanists to embody the highest principles of humanism, including mutual care and responsibility.
foundationbeyondbelief.org

Freedom From Religion Foundation
Works to educate the public on matters relating to nontheism, and to promote the constitutional principle of separation between church and state.
ffrf.org

Godless Perverts
Presents and promotes a positive view of sexuality without religion, by and for sex-positive atheists, agnostics, humanists, and other nonbelievers, through performance events, panel discussions, social gatherings, media productions, and other appropriate outlets.
godlessperverts.com

Grief Beyond Belief
Faith-free support for non-religious people grieving the death of a loved one.
facebook.com/faithfreegriefsupport

Hispanic American Freethinkers
An educational organization that serves as a resource and supports Hispanic freethinkers who promote the search for truth through science, rational thought, and critical thinking.
hafree.org

Humanist Association of Ireland
A community of people who believe in humanist principles and aspire to a fair, balanced, ethical and responsible secular society.
humanism.ie

Humanist Celebrants at the Humanist Society
Humanist Celebrants conduct Humanist, nonreligious, and interreligious weddings, commitment/same-sex unions, memorials, baby namings, and other life cycle ceremonies.
humanist-society.org/celebrants/

Jehovah's Witness Recovery
An online environment that promotes positive healing and recovery from the Watchtower Society of Jehovah's Witnesses.
jehovahswitnessrecovery.com

Kasese United Humanist Association
Promoting humanism and free thought in communities around the country, with special reference to the Western Uganda region.
kaseseunitedhumanistassociation.blogspot.com

LifeRing Secular Recovery
A worldwide network of individuals seeking to live in recovery from addiction to alcohol or to other non-medically indicated drugs. Sober, secular, and self-directed.
lifering.org

Military Association of Atheists and Freethinkers
Builds community for atheists and humanists in the military, and takes action to educate and train both the military and civilian community about atheism in the military and the issues facing them.
militaryatheists.org

National Federation of Atheist, Humanist and Secularist Student Societies
An association of atheist, humanist and secular student societies facilitated and supported by the British Humanist Association.
ahsstudents.org.uk

Pakistani Atheists and Agnostics
PAA is about rational thought, compassion, science, freedom, and education. They provide a forum for freethinkers in Pakistan to get together, share ideas and strive for common ambitions.
facebook.com/Pakistani.Atheists

Recovering From Religion

Learning how to live after questions, doubts, and changing beliefs is a journey. At Recovering From Religion they are intimately familiar with this path, and are here to help you to cross that bridge. Their passion is connecting others with support, resources, community, and most of all, hope.

recoveringfromreligion.org

Secular Coalition for America

Their mission is to increase the visibility of and respect for nontheistic viewpoints in the United States, and to protect and strengthen the secular character of our government as the best guarantee of freedom for all.

secular.org

Secular Student Alliance

Their mission is to empower secular students to proudly express their identity, build welcoming communities, promote secular values, and set a course for lifelong activism.

secularstudents.org

Secular Therapist Project

A confidential service matching nonbelievers looking for therapy with secular therapists: therapists who are nonbelievers or are committed to providing secular, evidence-based therapy that does not involve supernatural or religious elements. The service is confidential for both patients and therapists.

seculartherapy.org

Secular Woman

Their mission is to amplify the voice, presence, and influence of non-religious women.

secularwoman.org

Society for Humanistic Judaism

The congregational arm of the Humanistic Jewish movement in North America. The SHJ offers a meaningful opportunity for the celebration of cultural Judaism. It provides a pathway into the Jewish community for many unaffiliated Jews.

shj.org

The Sunday Assembly

A secular congregation that celebrates life.

sundayassembly.com

United Coalition of Reason

A nonprofit national organization that helps local nontheistic groups work together to achieve higher visibility, gain more members, and have a greater impact in their local areas.

unitedcor.org

ONLINE FORUMS/ RESOURCES/ SUPPORT NETWORKS

Atheist Nexus

The world's largest coalition of nontheists and nontheist communities.

atheistnexus.org

Atheists of Color: A List

A list of prominent atheists of color, organizations of atheists of color, and atheist organizations predominantly focused on and/or participated in by people of color.

the-orbit.net/greta/2011/03/21/atheists-of-color

Atheist Parents

Dedicated to helping parents worldwide to raise well-educated, thoughtful, ethical, socially responsible, environmentally aware, and most importantly, godless children.

atheistparents.org

Black Atheist Alliance
A Facebook forum where black atheists, agnostics, the nonreligious, and open minded believers can get together to express their views. All are welcome, regardless of your race or religious views.
facebook.com/groups/blackatheistalliance

ExChristian.net
Encouraging de-converting and former Christians.
exchristian.net

Grief Beyond Belief
Faith-free support for non-religious people grieving the death of a loved one.
facebook.com/faithfreegriefsupport

Grounded Parents
Skeptical parenting blog by a team of parents from a variety of backgrounds, some less traditional than others, some extraordinarily traditional.
groundedparents.com

No Longer Quivering
A gathering place for women escaping and healing from spiritual abuse. particular from the Quiverfull philosophy and lifestyle.
nolongerquivering.com

Present Moment Mindfulness
Mindfulness practice and science from a secular perspective. Podcasts, articles, meditation instructions and support, online practice circle, and more.
presentmomentmindfulness.com

Secular Cafe
A place for mostly secular people to socialize, support, and discuss religion, science, politics, etc.
secularcafe.org

South African Skeptics
An online skeptic community for and by South Africans.
skeptic.za.org

Spiritual Abuse Survivor Blogs Network
Supporting and promoting spiritual abuse survivors through individual blogging efforts.
patheos.com/blogs/nolongerquivering/spiritual-abuse-survivor-blogs-network

BLOGS/ BLOG NETWORKS

The Orbit
A diverse collective of atheist and nonreligious bloggers committed to social justice, within and outside the secular community. We provide a platform for writing, discussion, activism, collaboration, and community. This is my blogging site.
the-orbit.net

Greta Christina's Blog
Atheism, sex, politics, dreams, and whatever. Thinking out loud since 2005.
the-orbit.net/greta

Freethought Blogs
An open platform for freethought writers. They are skeptics and critics of dogma and authoritarianism: in addition, they recognize that the nonexistence of deities entails a greater commitment to human values, and in particular, an appreciation of human diversity and equality.
freethoughtblogs.com

Patheos Atheism
The Atheism channel of Patheos, the religious blog network. Home to many excellent atheist and humanist blogs.
patheos.com/atheist

Skepchick

A collection of smart and often sarcastic blogs focused on science and critical thinking. The original site was founded to discuss women's issues from a skeptical standpoint. The network now includes Queereka (LGBTQ issues), School of Doubt (education), Mad Art Lab, Teen Skepchick, Grounded Parents, and Skeptability (disability issues). There are also sites for speakers of Spanish, Swedish, and Norwegian.
skepchick.org

VIDEOBLOGS/PODCASTS/RADIO

Atheists Talk

Radio with a frankly atheist perspective. Hosted by Minnesota Atheists.
mnatheists.org/news-and-media/podcast

Dogma Debate

A fast-paced live talk radio show on topics from politics and religion to science and comedy.
dogmadebate.com

Freethought Radio & Podcast

Radio for the rest of us! Slightly irreverent views, news, music and interviews! By the Freedom From Religion Foundation.
ffrf.org/news/radio

Geeks Without God

No mystical energy field controls my destiny. Podcast.
geekswithoutgod.com

Free Mind TV

Atheism in the Arab world. A secular online media outlet and news TV station for the Middle East and the world.
free-mind.tv

The Humanist Hour

Podcast of the American Humanist Association.

thehumanist.com/multimedia/the-humanist-hour

Life, the Universe & Everything Else

A podcast promoting secular humanism and scientific skepticism, produced by the Winnipeg Skeptics.

lueepodcast.wordpress.com

Point of Inquiry

The Center for Inquiry's flagship podcast, where the brightest minds of our time sound off on all the things you're not supposed to talk about at the dinner table: science, religion, and politics.

pointofinquiry.org

The Thinking Atheist

Assume nothing. Question everything. And start thinking. Podcasts and videos by Seth Andrews.

thethinkingatheist.com

FILMS

A Better Life: An Exploration of Joy & Meaning in a World Without God

Creation

Hug an Atheist

Kumare

The Ledge

Letting Go of God

Marjoe

The Lord Is Not On Trial Here Today

Patriarchs and Penises: Sam Singleton, Atheist Evangelist

Sophia Investigates the Good News Club

BOOKS

African American Humanism: An Anthology, by Norm R. Allen, editor

African American Humanist Principles: Living and Thinking Like the Children of Nimrod, by Anthony B. Pinn

Atheism: A Reader, by S.T. Joshi

Atheism: A Very Short Introduction, by Julian Baggini

Atheism For Dummies, by Dale McGowan

Atheist Mind, Humanist Heart: Rewriting the Ten Commandments for the Twenty-first Century, by Lex Bayer and John Figdor

Atheist Voices of Minnesota: An Anthology of Personal Stories, by Bill Lehto, editor

A Better Life: 100 Atheists Speak Out on Joy & Meaning in a World Without God, by Chris Johnson

Black and Not Baptist: Nonbelief and Freethought in the Black Community, by Donald Barbera

The Black Humanist Experience: An Alternative to Religion, by Norm R. Allen

By These Hands: A Documentary History of African American Humanism, by Anthony B. Pinn

Caught in The Pulpit: Leaving Belief Behind, by Daniel C. Dennett

Confession of a Buddhist Atheist, by Stephen Batchelor

Comforting Thoughts About Death That Have Nothing to Do With God, by Greta Christina

Coming Out Atheist: How to Do It, How to Help Each Other, and Why, by Greta Christina

Creating Change Through Humanism, by Roy Speckhardt

Daylight Atheism, by Adam Lee

Deconverted: A Journey from Religion to Reason, by Seth Andrews

The Digital Cuttlefish: Omnibus, by Digital Cuttlefish

Disbelief 101: A Young Person's Guide to Atheism, by S.C. Hitchcock

Doubt: A History: The Great Doubters and Their Legacy of Innovation from Socrates and Jesus to Thomas Jefferson and Emily Dickinson, by Jennifer Michael Hecht

The Ebony Exodus Project: Why Some Black Women Are Walking Out on Religion—And Others Should Too, by Candace R. M. Gorham, LPC

The End of God-Talk: An African American Humanist Theology, by Anthony B. Pinn

Facing Oblivion: Essays on Life, Death and Grieving from a Nonbeliever, by J.D. Brucker

Freethinkers: A History of American Secularism, by Susan Jacoby

From Apostle to Apostate: The Story of the Clergy Project, by Catherine Dunphy

Generation Atheist, by Dan Riley

Godless: How an Evangelical Preacher Became One of America's Leading Atheists, by Dan Barker

Godless Americana: Race & Religious Rebels, by Sikivu Hutchinson

The Good Atheist: Living a Purpose-Filled Life Without God, by Dan Barker

The Good Book: A Humanist Bible, by A.C. Grayling

Good Without God: What a Billion Nonreligious People Do Believe, by Greg Epstein

Growing Up Godless: A Parent's Guide to Raising Kids Without Religion, by Deborah Mitchell

The Happy Atheist, by PZ Myers

Hope After Faith: An Ex-Pastor's Journey from Belief to Atheism, by Jerry DeWitt

How Do You Know It's True? by Hy Ruchlis

Icons of Unbelief: Atheists, Agnostics, and Secularists, S.T. Joshi, editor

I'm a Freethinker, by Courtney Lynn

I'm An Atheist And That's Ok, by Courtney Lynn

In Faith and In Doubt: How Religious Believers and Nonbelievers Can Create Strong Marriages and Loving Families, by Dale McGowan

It Is Ok To Be A Godless Me, by Courtney Lynn

Judaism for Everyone... Without Dogma, by Bernardo Sorj

Just Pretend: A Freethought Book for Children, by Dan Barker and Alma Cuebas

Leaving the Fold: A Guide for Former Fundamentalists and Others Leaving Religion, by Marlene Winell

Life, Sex and Ideas: The Good Life without God, by A.C. Grayling

Living the Secular Life: New Answers to Old Questions, by Phil Zuckerman

Maybe Right, Maybe Wrong, by Dan Barker

Meditations for the Humanist: Ethics for a Secular Age, by A.C. Grayling

Mistakes Were Made (But Not by Me): Why We Justify Foolish Beliefs, Bad Decisions, and Hurtful Acts, by Carol Tavris and Elliot Aronson

Mom, Dad, I'm an Atheist: The Guide to Coming Out as a Non-Believer, by David G. McAfee

Moral Combat: Black Atheists, Gender Politics, and the Values Wars, by Sikivu Hutchinson

Mortality, by Christopher Hitchens

Nonbeliever Nation: The Rise of Secular Americans, by David Niose

Nothing: Something to Believe in, by Nica Lalli

Older Than the Stars, by Karen C. Fox and Nancy Davis

The Only Prayer I'll Ever Pray: Let My People Go, by Donald R. Wright

Parenting Beyond Belief: On Raising Caring, Ethical Kids Without Religion, by Dale McGowan

Parenting Without God: How to Raise Moral, Ethical and Intelligent Children, Free from Religious Dogma, by Dan Arel

Raising Freethinkers: A Practical Guide for Parenting Beyond Belief, by Dale McGowan

Secular Meditation: 32 Practices for Cultivating Inner Peace, Compassion, and Joy, by Rick Heller

Sex & God: How Religion Distorts Sexuality, by Darrel W. Ray

Sketti Tales: An Adventure Through Space and Time, by Courtney Lynn

Society Without God: What the Least Religious Nations Can Tell Us About Contentment, by Phil Zuckerman

Through Space And Time, by Courtney Lynn

The Unbelievers: The Evolution of Modern Atheism, by S.T. Joshi

Voices of Unbelief: Documents from Atheists and Agnostics, by Dale McGowan, editor

What is Humanism, and Why Does it Matter? (Studies in Humanist Thought and Praxis), by Anthony B. Pinn

Why Are You Atheists So Angry? 99 Things That Piss off the Godless, by Greta Christina

Writing God's Obituary: How a Good Methodist Became a Better Atheist, by Anthony B. Pinn

The Young Atheist's Survival Guide: Helping Secular Students Thrive, by Hemant Mehta

Young, Sick, and Invisible: A Skeptic's Journey with Chronic Illness, by Ania Bula

ENDNOTES

What Does It All Mean?

Chapter 1: Caring about Reality: Why It Matters What We Don't Believe

1. Author's personal records. The conversation happened on Facebook years ago, and I copied the words down directly at the time.

Chapter 8: Living Each Day as If If Were Your Last

1. The Simpsons, " C.E.D'oh!," March 16, 2003.

Doing the Right Thing

Chapter 9: Two Different Ways to Be a Good Person

1. Tavris, Carol, and Elliot Aronson. Mistakes Were Made (but Not by Me): Why We Justify Foolish Beliefs, Bad Decisions, and Hurtful Acts. Houghton Mifflin Harcourt, 2007.
2. Stanford Prison Experiment, http://www.prisonexp.org/
3. McCleod, Saul. "The Milgram Experiment." Simply Psychology, 2007, http://www.simplypsychology.org/milgram.html

Chapter 10: Good Intentions

1. Ostropoler, Hershele, August 4, 2012 (12:30 am), comment on John Scalzi, "Readercon, Harassment, Etc" by John Scalzi, *Whatever*, July 31, 2012, http://whatever.scalzi.com/2012/07/31/readercon-harassment-etc/#comment-346433

Chapter 11: Starting with the Assumption That I'm Wrong

1. Bula, Ania, "Ableism Challenge," on *Alyssa and Ania 'Splain You a Thing*, June 14, 2015, http://the-orbit.net/splainyouathing/2015/06/14/ableism-challenge/

Chapter 14: Consent

1. Friedman, Jaclyn, and Jessica Valenti. *Yes Means Yes!: Visions of Female Sexual Power and A World Without Rape*. Seal Press, 2008.
2. Watson, Rebecca, "Twitter Users Sad To Hear They May Be Rapists," on *Skepchick*, December 18, 2012, http://skepchick.org/2012/12/twitter-users-sad-to-hear-they-may-be-rapists/
3. Carey, Anna. "Depressing but not surprising: how the Magdalene Laundries got away with it." New Stateman, July 17, 2013, http://www.newstatesman.com/religion/2013/07/depressing-not-surprising-how-magdalene-laundries-got-away-it

Chapter 15: Why Atheism Needs Social Justice—And How That Might Work

1. Christina, Greta. *Why Are You Atheists So Angry? 99 Things That Piss Off the Godless.* Pitchstone Publishing, 2012.
2. Gorham, Candace R.M. *The Ebony Exodus Project: Why Some Black Women Are Walking Out on Religion—and Others Should Too.* Pitchstone Publishing, 2013.

Chapter 17: The Part about Black Lives Mattering Where White People Shut Up and Listen

1. McIntosh, Peggy. "White Privilege: Unpacking the Invisible Knapsack," *Independent School,* Winter 1990, http://ted.coe.wayne.edu/ele3600/mcintosh.html
2. Miller, Joyce. "Product Review: The Invisible Backpack of White Privilege from L.L. Bean," McSweeney's Internet Tendency, December 18, 2014, http://www.mcsweeneys.net/articles/product-review-the-invisible-backpack-of-white-privilege-from-ll-bean
3. Christina, Greta. "Atheists of Color—A List," on *Greta Christina's Blog,* originally published March 21, 2011, subsequently updated multiples times, http://the-orbit.net/greta/2011/03/21/atheists-of-color/

Chapter 18: Trans People and Basic Human Respect

1. Zvan, Stephanie, What Is a Blogger to Do?, on *Almost Diamonds*, August 7, 2015, http://the-orbit.net/almostdiamonds/2015/08/07/what-is-a-blogger-to-do/
2. Martin, Judith. Miss Manners' Guide to Excruciatingly Correct Behavior (Freshly Updated), Page 128. W. W. Norton & Company, 2011.
3. "Injustice at Every Turn: A Report of the National Transgender Discrimination Survey," National Center for Transgender Equality and National Gay and Lesbian Task Force, 2011
4. "Transgender Rates of Violence," FORGE, October 2012. "International Day Against Homophobia and Transphobia Report 2014," Transgender Violence Tracking Portal, 2014.

Chapter 19: Sex Work and a Catch-22

1. Reed, Natalie, Catches-22, on *Sincerely, Natalie Reed*, Febrrary 27, 2012, http://freethoughtblogs.com/nataliereed/2012/02/27/catches-twenty-two/

Tough Stuff: Sickness, Suffering, Death

Chapter 23: Mental Illness and Responsibility

1. Christina, Greta, Richard Hermann Muelder, 1933-2012, on *Greta Christina's Blog*, October 12, 2012, http://the-orbit.net/greta/2012/10/12/richard-hermann-muelder-1933-2012/
2. Churchland, Patricia S. *Touching a Nerve: The Self as Brain*, pp 168-194. W.W. Norton & Company, 2013.

Chapter 28: Some Comforting Thoughts about Death, and When They Don't Work

1. Boyles, Salynn, "Patients Who Rely on Religion to Cope Are More Likely to Have Aggressive Medical Care," *WebMD Health News*, March 17, 2009.
2. Grief Beyond Belief, facebook.com/faithfreegriefsupport
3. Grief Beyond Belief, griefbeyondbelief.org.
4. Myers, PZ. Why do we die?, on *Pharyngula*, January 13, 2015, http://freethoughtblogs.com/pharyngula/2015/01/13/why-do-we-die/
5. ethereal, January 14, 2015 (7:42 am), comment on Myers on Death, Evolution, and "Comforting Thoughts About Death That Have Nothing to Do with God" by Greta Christina, *Greta Christina's Blog*, January 13, 2015, http://the-orbit.net/greta/2015/01/13/pz-myers-comforting-thoughts/#comment-620

Chapter 30: Dealing with Death in an Unjust World

1. Juzwiak, Rich, and Aleksander Chan, *Unarmed People of Color Killed by Police, 1999-2014*, on Gawker, December 8, 2014, http://gawker.com/unarmed-people-of-color-killed-by-police-1999-2014-1666672349
2. African American Policy Forum, "Say Her Name," http://www.aapf.org/sayhername/

Playing Well with Others: Believers and Other Atheists

Chapter 34: How Confrontation Can Open Doors

1. Clint, Ed. Transfaith, The New Atheist Interfaith. Talk at Secular Student Alliance 2011 Annual Leadership Conference, uploaded to YouTube on Aug 18, 2011, https://www.youtube.com/watch?v=VNKokaFxYL8

Chapter 37: Compassion for the Religious

1. Christina, Greta. *Why Are You Atheists So Angry? 99 Things That Piss Off the Godless.* Pitchstone Publishing, 2012.

Chapter 39: Is It Okay to Mock Religion?

1. Ola, quoted in Is It Okay to Mock Religion?, on *Greta Christina's Blog*, May 28, 2009, http://the-orbit.net/greta/2009/05/28/is-it-okay-to-mock-religion/

Chapter 44: Why Do There Need to Be "Special Interest" Atheist Groups?

1. Kunerth, Jeff, "Black atheists search for sense of belonging," *Orlando Sentinel*, March 22, 2013, http://articles.orlandosentinel.com/2013-03-22/features/os-black-atheists-20130322_1_atheists-black-church-black-community
2. "About Us: Ex-Muslims of North America," Ex-Muslims of North America, http://www.exmna.org/about-us/
3. "Secular Woman FAQ," Secular Woman, http://www.secularwoman.org/faq/
4. Gaudette, Bridget R., Shades of Black Atheism #3: Mandisa Thomas, on *Friendly Atheist*, January 15, 2013, http://www.patheos.com/blogs/friendlyatheist/2013/01/15/shades-of-black-atheism-3-mandisa-thomas/?repeat=w3tc

5. Hutchinson, Sikivu, Atheism has a big race problem that no one's talking about, Washington Post, June 16, 2014, https://www.washingtonpost.com/posteverything/wp/2014/06/16/blacks-are-even-discriminated-against-by-atheists/

Chapter 45: Policing Our Own

1. Christina, Greta, "Policing Their Own," on *Greta Christina's Blog*, May 8, 2013, multiple citations with links, http://the-orbit.net/greta/2013/05/08/policing-their-own/

Chapter 46: More Rational Than Thou

1. Galef, Julia, "The Straw Vulcan: Hollywood's Illogical View of Logical Decision-Making," talk at Skepticon 4, uploaded to YouTube Nov 25, 2011, https://www.youtube.com/watch?v=tLgNZ9aTEwc

The Good Life: Sex, Love, Pleasure, and Joy

Chapter 51: My Vision for a Sexual World

1. Sacks, Oliver. *Musicophilia: Tales of Music and the Brain*. Alfred A. Knopf, 2007.

Chapter 52: "Nothing to Do with Destined Perfection": An Atheist View of Love

1. Minchin, Tim. Love is nothing to do with destined perfection. "If I Didn't Have You," live at the Secret Policeman's Ball 2008, uploaded onto YouTube Oct 7, 2008, https://www.youtube.com/watch?v=Gaid72fqzNE

Chapter 53: Intransitive Gratitude: Feeling Thankful in a Godless World

1. Fellowship of Freethought Dallas, "Thanks for Skepticon," uploaded to YouTube Nov 20, 2011, https://www.youtube.com/watch?v=53j_pNgEfy0

CREDITS

"Consent," "Permanent Struggle," previously unpublished.

"Skepticism as a Discipline," "Mental Illness and Responsibility," "My Body is the Knife: The Reality of Medical Uncertainty," "What Do You Say to Grieving Non Believers?" "Is It Okay to Persuade Believers Out of Religion?" "Trekkie Religion and Secular Judaism: How Do We Use the Good Stuff From Religion?" originally published on AlterNet.

"My Vision for a Sexual World," originally published on The Blowfish Blog.

"Why Atheism Needs Social Justice—And How That Might Work," "The Problem of Nuance in a Wonderful and Terrible World," "What Would Happen If We All Came Out?" "What Does Religion Provide?" "Infighting Versus Healthy Debate," "Atheism and Sensuality," originally published in Free Inquiry.

"Caring About Reality: Why What We Don't Believe Matters," "The Uses of Irrationality, and its Limitations," "The Sweet Mystery of Life," "Atheist Meaning in a Small, Brief Life," "Why Are We Here?" "The Human Animal," "Living Each Day As If It Were Your Last," "Two Different Ways to Be a Good

Person," "Intention and Magic," "Why 'Yes, But' Is the Wrong Response to Misogyny," "Sex Work and a Catch-22," "Bad Luck and the Comfort of Reason," "Everything Happens For a Reason," "Atheist Funerals," "Atheists in the Pride Parade: Churlishness and Integrity," "Atheism and Friendship," "Is It Okay to Mock Religion?" "Atheism and Patience," "What Are The Goals of the Atheist Movement?" "The Power to Name Ourselves: Why I Don't Give a Damn If You Call Yourself Atheist, Agnostic, Humanist, Skeptic, Freethinker, Secular, or What," "Why Do There Need to Be 'Special Interest' Atheist Groups?" "Policing Our Own," "More Rational Than Thou," "'There Is No Atheist Movement': Why I'm Done With Dictionary Atheism," "Atheist Thoughts on a Life Well-Lived," "To Give Itself Pleasure: An Atheist View of Sexual Transcendence," "An Atheist View of Love," "Intransitive Gratitude: Feeling Thankful in a Godless World," "For No Good Reason," "'Ya Gotta Reach For Your Dreams'," "Letting the World Surprise You," "Part of the Show," originally published on Greta Christina's Blog.

"Should We Care What Other People Think?" "The Part About Black Lives Mattering Where White People Shut Up and Listen," "Trans People and Basic Human Respect," "The Pros and Cons of Caring About Other People," "How Humanism Helps With Depression—Except When It Doesn't," "Dealing with Death in an Unjust World," "Atheism in a Shitstorm," "How Confrontation Can Open Doors," "Compassion for the Religious," "Imposter Syndrome, and What It Means to Be An Adult," "Work/Life Balance," "In Praise of Frivolity," originally published in The Humanist.

"An Atheist View of Sexual Ethics," given as talk in various forms on multiple occasions.

Portions of "Comforting Thoughts About Death: A Quick Summary, and Thoughts About When They Don't Work" previously unpublished; other portions originally published on Greta Christina's Blog.

Portions of "A Less Simplistic View of Evil: The Jasmine Storyline in 'Angel,' And Why People Do Awful Awful Things," "'There Has to be Something More': Atheism and Yearning," "Does Social Justice Mean Mission Drift for Atheism?" "Diplomacy and Accommodationism Are Not The Same Thing," incorporated into other chapters, originally published on Greta Christina's Blog.

ABOUT THE AUTHOR

Greta Christina is author of *Why Are You Atheists So Angry? 99 Things That Piss Off the Godless*, *Coming Out Atheist: How to Do It, How to Help Each Other, and Why*, *Comforting Thoughts about Death That Have Nothing to Do with God*, and *Bending: Dirty Kinky Stories About Pain, Power, Religion, Unicorns, & More*. She blogs at Greta Christina's Blog, one of the most widely-read and well-respected blogs in the atheist blogosphere. She is one of the co-founders of The Orbit at the-orbit.net, a diverse collective of atheist and nonreligious bloggers committed to social justice, and is a regular contributor to *AlterNet*, *Salon*, *Free Inquiry*, and *The Humanist*. Her writing has appeared in numerous magazines and newspapers, including *Ms.*, *Penthouse*, *Skeptical Inquirer*, and the *Chicago Sun-Times*. She is editor of the *Best Erotic Comics* anthology series and of *Paying For It: A Guide by Sex Workers for Their Clients*. She has been writing professionally since 1989, on topics including atheism, skepticism, sexuality and sex-positivity, LGBT issues, politics, culture, and whatever crosses her mind. She is on the speakers' bureaus of the Secular Student Alliance and the Center for Inquiry. She tweets @GretaChristina. She lives in San Francisco with her wife, Ingrid.